ASSERTIVENESS FOR MANAGERS

ASSERTIVENESS FOR MANAGERS
Learning effective skills for managing people

Diana Cawood, B.A., M.Sc.

Self-Counsel Press
(*a division of*)
International Self-Counsel Press Ltd.
Canada   U.S.A.

Printed in Canada

First edition: April, 1983
Second edition: January, 1988
Third edition: March, 1992

Canadian Cataloguing in Publication Data
Cawood, Diana
      Assertiveness for managers
      (Self-counsel business series)
      ISBN 0-88908-996-5
      1. Assertiveness (Psychology) 2. Management—Psychological aspects.
I. Title   II. Series.
HF5549.C38 1992 658.4'092 C91-091822-8

Cover photograph by Terry Guscott, ATN Visuals, Vancouver, B.C.

Self-Counsel Press
(*a division of*)
International Self-Counsel Press Ltd.
Head and Editorial Office
1481 Charlotte Road
North Vancouver, British Columbia V7J 1H1

U.S. Address
1704 N. State Street
Bellingham, Washington 98225

CONTENTS

CHARTS

WORKSHEETS

SAMPLES

PREFACE

a. HOW THIS BOOK GOT STARTED

I developed the ideas in this book over a period of two or three years while running workshops for managers on the topic of assertive skills. It was only within the last few years that the workshops could actually be called "Assertive Skills for Managers." Prior to that the topic was couched in other terms, "Communication Skills," "Guidelines," etc. It is only recently that more and more managers are publicly "asserting their rights" to learn the skills that work more effectively in today's changing world.

The participants in these workshops represented a wide variety of businesses and professions. The specifics of many of their problem situations were different but there were always several common themes. Many of the examples used in this book were drawn from their actual experiences as we worked on them in the workshops.

b. HOW TO USE THIS BOOK

This book contains ideas and explanations about assertive communication as well as examples and exercises to let you practice the techniques. Although you will achieve better results if you do the exercises, you can still gain by reading the book through for the ideas and explanations.

Read and work through it slowly. When you finish a chapter, put it aside for a few days or a week and watch for the ideas expressed to be played out in your day-to-day life. Take this time to practice one or two things only. The ideas in this book suggest a communication style with which most of us are not familiar or particularly comfortable. We've all spent years developing our present styles; it will take some time to unlearn old habits of responding and learn new ways to listen and express ourselves. Adults hate to make mistakes with something as basic as "talking," but when you are learning a new skill you still have to start from the beginning, go slowly, and suffer a few failures.

As you integrate one chapter into your day-to-day life, try the next chapter and do the same thing: watch, practice, and assess results.

The exercises provide a way to check your own understanding of the material and you are encouraged to take the time to do them. Suggested answers for the exercises are in the Appendix, but there are many possible answers for each exercise.

One particularly useful way the material in this book has been used is when all members of the same group (office, department, company, etc.) start to learn the skills at the same time. Then the new language of the skills fits everyone's frame of reference and each can support the other with appropriate feedback.

ACKNOWLEDGMENTS

I thank Dena, my daughter, and David, my ex-husband. I have learned many lessons with both of them about clarity, courage, and care.

> "...Love and I had the wit to win:
> We drew a circle that took him in."

A few lines from an unremembered poem of many years ago. Its spirit underlies much of the message in this book.

1
WHY DO MANAGERS NEED ASSERTIVE SKILLS?

a. CAN'T GET TO FIRST BASE*

Costello: That's what I want to find out. I want you to tell me the names of the players.

Abbott: I'm telling you. Who's on first. What's on second. I Don't Know's on third.

Costello: You know the fellows' names?

Abbott: Yes.

Costello: Well, who's playing first?

Abbott: Yes.

Costello: I mean the fellow's name on first base.

Abbott: Who.

Costello: The fellow playing first base for St. Louis.

Abbott: Who.

Costello: The guy on first base.

Abbott: Who's on first.

Costello: What are you asking me for?

This is a familiar routine from Abbott and Costello, but also an all too familiar routine for many managers.

Managers get trapped into going around and around the same dialogue again and again with their colleagues, subordinates, and bosses.

Some managers are too passive. They defer their views, withhold their feelings, suppress their rights, and let others manipulate the discussion in the same old unproductive cycle. Other managers are too aggressive. They assume they are right, that only their views and feelings count, and, through intimidation and domination, they perpetuate the same old unproductive cycle with others.

When managers are passive or aggressive, no new information is exchanged. No progress is made on the problem at hand. Like Costello, you find yourself "back on third again" and again!

Abbott: Who's on first.

Costello: I don't know.

Abbott: He's on third. We're not talking about him.

Costello: How did I get on third base?

Abbott: You mentioned his name.

Costello: If I mentioned the third baseman's name, who is playing third?

Abbott: No. Who's playing first.

Costello: Stay off of first, will you?

Abbott: Well, what do you want me to do?

Costello: Okay, what's the guy's name on first?

Abbott: What's on second.

Costello: I'm not asking you who's on second.

Abbott: Who's on first.

Costello: I don't know.

Abbott: He's on third.

Costello: There I go back on third again.

Funny and entertaining? Yes. Each time Abbott and Costello cycle through their

---

*"Who's On First?" script copyright by the estate of Abbott and Costello. Reprinted by permission.

time-consuming, unproductive pattern, they raise their voices, harden their tone, tighten their body posture, and sweat a little more. Funny to watch as a comic routine, but not funny when the same routine is happening to you as a manager in real life.

Assertive skills help you break the pattern. Assertive skills help you get to "first base" and solve real problems rather than re-create old frustrations. Assertive skills help you minimize defensive, aggressive reactions which block true communication.

As a manager, you have probably noticed the increasing availability of assertive skills workshops in the marketplace. There's a reason for this. Many people have a need to find new, more effective ways to articulate their choices and to justify and deal with the issues that changes in values and information have generated.

Your need to break out of old patterns is no different. It is, if anything, more critical because your role as a manager demands that you "manage" the process between person and person and between person and job. You cannot afford to have this process become blocked, unproductive, or a "funny" routine.

Consider just three of the new challenges you are confronting as a manager for which you need assertive skills:

- Reaching the "new individualists" swelling the work force
- Processing increased information
- Coaching the careers of those you manage

b. NEW DAYS, NEW WAYS: TODAY'S WORKERS

Many of the people you manage belong to the generation of workers known as the new individualists, who bring with them values and expectations that do not conform to the old tradition of hard work and respect for authority.

These men and women have legitimized a variety of job styles and life styles, including shared jobs, home-based jobs, different modifications of flextime and four-day work weeks, and roles for househusbands, multiperson "families," and single-parent executives.

The nature of work has changed

Workers no longer respond to an authoritarian style of management

As well, many workers are trying to redefine organizational life with corporate daycare programs and paternity leave.

They rely less on formal authority. They value, instead, the right to be heard and to have their input respected. How would you respond to this unsolicited comment from one of your new engineering recruits:

> I've been giving some thought to your inventory control system. I think it's ineffective in keeping inventories at optimal levels.

Or this question from a planning assistant:

> Why do we worry about meeting their deadline? You know they never use the report to make their decision.

They expect their work to *mean something*. They will no longer accept unquestioned those jobs that cannot offer challenge and a sense of closure, of doing something.

The surveys of Daniel Yankelovich confirm that the new individualists cross all worker ranks — blue collar and white collar. Young blue collar workers state their expectations more bluntly with demands for "less compulsory overtime, better working conditions, getting the foreman off my back, a product worth pride, more leisure, and so forth. Or they may act them out in wildcat strikes, absenteeism, job-hopping, and even sabotage."*

They affirm their own personal values as opposed to anyone else's — including management's. Many are hard workers, good workers, insightful, creative, responsible — *on the job*. But, they'll let you know quite unequivocally that intrusions into their private lives or personal time are not part of the bargain.

How do you respond to an unexpected (at least to you) refusal by one of your accountants to come in on Saturday morning?

Or, have you ever been as bewildered as this manager who states:

> He turned us down. But so have two others since. This is a top job, but people won't move around the country the way they used to.

---

*Louis Banks, "Here Come the Individualists," *Harvard Magazine*, September-October, 1977.

These new individualists are often very articulate, clear thinkers. How do you respond to the challenges of their demands for equal authority on matters of input, for meaningfulness in their jobs, and for personal as well as organizational lives?

Old patterns of confrontation, outright denial, or passive ignoring will not do. Assertive skills will help.

c. FASTER PACE, SMALLER SPACE

As a manager, have you ever said to yourself:

I used to have time to think, to kind of mull things over. Now, the revisions are almost back on my desk before I get back.

As a manager, has anyone ever said to you:

If you can't give us the figures now, you know Blentel will come in with a quote of their own. We can't wait.

As a manager, have you ever demanded of someone else:

I don't care how you get through it all! I need to know by 5:00.

You're aware of some of the changes brought about by the increased pace at which we work, the instant information available, and the technological innovations. Are you also aware of how these changes have put demands on your communication skills — especially your assertive skills?

- You feel the stress of pressures to make faster decisions, assessing growing amounts of data. You need skills to cut through to the heart of the problem quickly in ways that will nurture and maintain the cooperation and respect of coworkers.

- You feel the stress of increased, often instant, visibility when you are plugged in (sometimes in color) "live" across the continent or your message is printed in branch offices across the

seas at the same time as you speak. You need skills to articulate your thoughts and feelings in ways that are spontaneously right, when you no longer have time to work yourself up for a presentation.

- You feel the stress of managing technicians whose work is more and more of a mystery to you. You need skills to ask questions in ways that do not undermine your self-respect.

d. CAREER CRUNCH: CAREER COACH

You and your employees are part of the career crunch of the 1990s. Employees want to know where and how they will move in their careers because of —

- (a) shifting values,
- (b) changing roles in society,
- (c) technological breakthroughs, and
- (d) job squeezes up the ladder.

To be an effective manager today you have to play a new role: career coach.

But I chat with my employees when we do our yearly performance review. Isn't that enough?

I've always said they can come and see me any time. What more can I do?

Shouldn't *they* know what they want to do?

What's *your* response to the role of coach?

- Are you aware of the concerns that arise at different career stages?

- Do you know how to create appropriate opportunities for multiple career options?

- Can you facilitate the information-gathering process as employees assess opportunities and obstacles?

In effect, you have to be able to act as a catalyst — to present alternatives, to give information, to listen, to support — not to legislate. The career decisions and the consequences ultimately rest with the individual employee — not you, the manager.

You need skills to manage this process of discussion, dilemma, and decision while neither taking over responsibility for the decision nor opting out because it's not your job.

Assertive skills can give you the confidence to initiate career discussions with your employees, to listen, and to respond in an appropriately supportive, yet non-directive, way.

You are the coach; your employee is the player.

e. BACK ON THIRD AGAIN or HAVEN'T WE BEEN HERE BEFORE?

Yes. We've been here before. This time let's explore some of the unproductive patterns you experience in your day-to-day life as a manager. How many times have you been "back on third" in your office? Are there situations that trigger the same old responses again and again where you can't get to first base?

Here are a few examples to start you thinking:

Old-timer cynic

Every time I introduce a new policy or a change of procedure to my staff, one guy, who's been with us about 31 years — and I'm sure he resents working for me — always starts in with the same old gripes and criticisms about how it's never going to work. I get hooked in justifying and explaining and finally just cut him off by laying down the law.

Meeting manic

I've got a super young rep in my department. She's full of ideas and has good insight on our market problems. The trouble is she takes over at every meeting, launching forth with a full scale analysis and report. No one else gets a chance to say anything. I don't want to cut her off because I'm afraid she'll shut up altogether then. I need her ideas but...

Policy pusher

I'm a bank manager and we have a policy not to cash checks for people who do not have accounts with us. Almost every day one of my staff runs into trouble with this and calls me in on it. I feel my staff should handle it, but we're always under time pressure so I always go talk to the customer. The whole discussion escalates until we're both mad. I'm getting to the point where I don't even care if the customer gets mad. I just wish I could handle it better so I wouldn't waste my time.

Silent saboteurs

We have to make a decision in our office about something. I call my staff in and ask for their ideas; no one speaks up. Same thing every time. I finally make the decision. They say nothing. Then, when it's too late, when we've set the wheels in motion, I start to get all kinds of flak about it being a bad idea. Why don't they speak up when I ask them?

Travelogue monologue

I love my clients. I really do. I need them to keep coming back, but I don't need them to come back to give me a day-by-day, dinner-by-dinner account of their holidays. Like yesterday, for an hour and twenty minutes I heard about Mrs. Holloway's trip to Mexico and had to look at her pictures. I haven't got time to listen. I don't even want to listen. But I do, every time.

WORKSHEET #1
CAN'T GET TO FIRST BASE

These are the ways I get hooked into repeating unproductive patterns:

1. _____

_____

_____

_____

2. _____

_____

_____

_____

3. _____

_____

_____

_____

4. _____

_____

_____

_____

You can probably see yourself back on third as you think of some of your day-to-day encounters. Use the space provided in Worksheet #1 to describe situations in which you seem to be repeating the same old, time-wasting, unproductive patterns.

The assertive skills you learn in this book will give you a way out — a way to break the cycle, a way to get to first base.

For further reading on the issues discussed, see:

Kanter, Rosabeth Moss. *When Giants Learn to Dance: Mastering the Challenges of Strategy, Management, and Careers in the 1990's.* New York: Simon and Schuster, 1989.

Yankelovich, Daniel. *New Rules.* Toronto: Bantam Books, 1982.

2
WHAT IS ASSERTIVE BEHAVIOR?

a. ASSESS YOURSELF

You're ready to get the definition straight about assertive behavior — to find out what the assumptions, the rights, and goals are. This section will do that. You'll also compare assertive behavior with "the others" — passive behavior and aggressive behavior — so that you will easily recognize the differences in your own style and in the style of those around you.

But, first, gather some data on your understanding of assertive skills. Worksheet #2 will help you assess yourself. How well can you discriminate between assertive, passive, and aggressive statements?

The situations describe common events that many managers encounter in their day-to-day interactions with those above them, those below them, and those with whom they work side by side.

There is no numerical scoring for the assessment in Worksheet #2. However, with the key at the end of this chapter, you can assess your own understanding of effective assertive statements. Note those with which you had trouble. Many examples will be given later showing how to make assertive statements for these situations.

b. THE DEFINITION OF ASSERTIVENESS

1. The give

Assertive behavior is a *direct, honest,* and *appropriate* expression of your thoughts, feelings, needs or rights without undue anxiety.

Direct: Your behavior is unswerving. Your message is clearly focused and natural, i.e., nonjudgmental. You don't beat around the bush. You don't "repackage" your message or manipulate others.

> I'd like to be a member of the task force on productivity improvement. I think my experience with the changes in production scheduling will be helpful to the team.

Honest: Your behavior is congruent. All signals match. Your words, your gestures, and your feelings are all saying the same thing.

> (With direct eye contact as you speak; relaxed body posture.) I'd prefer you didn't ask me to cover for you. I don't like to lie.

Appropriate: Your behavior takes into account the rights and feelings of others as well as your own. The time and place are right.

> You know your staff worked late last night. But the office is in a mess this morning — dirty cups, open files, etc. You're expecting a client.

> You say nothing now — but quickly and quietly begin to pick up the worst of it.

> If your staff worked late, they'll resent being hit with criticism on maintenance issues first thing — no matter how assertively you say it. You're likely to initiate an explosive reaction (which you don't have time to handle right

WORKSHEET #2
ASSESS YOURSELF

After reading the statement following each situation, decide if you think the statement is an example of assertive, passive, or aggressive behavior. In the space provided beside each statement, indicate your choice with the appropriate symbol.

Assertive (+)　　　**Passive (-)**　　　**Aggressive (x)**

SITUATION	YOU SAY:	STATEMENT IS:
1.You know your staff worked late last night. But the office is in a mess this morning — dirty cups, ashtrays, open files, etc. You're expecting a client.	"Hey, clean this place up. What do you think Astel's going to think of this?"	
2.A colleague has asked you to cover for her while she takes a few extra hours after lunch. You don't want her to ask you to do this.	"Oh sure. Well, I hope no one comes looking for you."	
3.You'd like to be a member of the productivity improvement task force just being formed by your boss.	"Sounds great! Good move. We could use some new ideas on productivity."	
4.One of your support staff has asked for Thursday off because her brother will be in town on that day. You're hitting tight deadlines and need her.	"I'd like to let you do it, but I won't."	
5.You like the way one of your staff handled a particularly difficult customer.	"Nobody's going to get the best of you today, are they?"	
6.The regional manager has just called to tell you the manager's meeting has been rescheduled for 1:30 this afternoon instead of 10:00 this morning. You have a meeting planned with a key supplier at 2:30.	"I guess it'll be okay. I'll work something out."	
7.During a routine staff meeting two members keep up their own low dialogue while another is giving her report.	"Quiet, you guys. You're going to need these figures, too."	
8.A fellow manager has just made a sarcastic remark to you at lunch over your success with getting your budget approved.	"Yeah, some might think so."	

SITUATION	YOU SAY:	STATEMENT IS:
9. The client for a big project has just told you your proposal is not competitive and you may lose the bid.	"We're giving you our best prices. No one can do it for less."	
10. One of your staff has just revealed in exasperation that you never listen to any of their ideas.	"Yes, I do."	
11. You've been talking to a fellow manager on the telephone for quite some time. You'd like to end the conversation.	"Look, I have to go. I've got a call waiting."	
12. Your boss has the habit of double checking what you tell him or figures you submit.	"Don't you trust me? I took a lot of time with it."	
13. One of your employees has interrupted you again, asking for something that could have waited.	You say nothing and get up to get it. It's easier than starting a big scene.	
14. Your word processing supervisor has just started telling you about what a rough day she's had with the staff.	"You mean, they're having trouble with the new equipment, is that it?"	
15. The regional manager has called to tell you what a great job you did on getting the new inventory control system in place.	"It's still not perfect. There are a few things I've got to work out yet."	
16. Your bookkeeper is having trouble balancing this month's accounts. You take a look at it.	"Why do you separate the expenses for each salesperson?"	
17. You want your new office supervisor to take more responsibility with the staff. He's come to you with problems over holiday schedules.	"The policy regarding holidays states that no holiday time can be carried over to the next year."	
18. In a meeting with the other managers, you present your views regarding the coming layoffs.	"I'm sorry, I can't agree with you. Don't you think it would be better if we offered relocation counselling?"	

10

now) and they'd be right. They would not be reacting to your criticism per se, but the fact that you have not been sensitive to their need for recognition and right to feel tired.

Later, in a discussion that is *not linked* to either overtime or the impending arrival of clients, you can deal with standards for office clean up.

2. And take

Assertive behavior is *interactive*. Equally important to your ability to give an assertive message is your ability to take in what others say or feel without reacting in ways that deny them the rights to their thoughts or feelings.

You can listen attentively to disappointments, dilemmas, or expectations from others without starting up your own internal dialogue (e.g., "how am I going to handle this one?" or "if I let him know...").

You can listen to anger or criticism from others without being "hooked in" to react in the same manner (anger begets anger) or with defensive denials.

Example

One of your staff has revealed with exasperation that you never listen to any of their ideas. You say:

> You mean I don't give credit to your input, is that it?

> or

> You're saying you'd like more involvement around here, is that what you mean?

> or

> You mean I'm not available enough, is that it?

> or

> You seem to be pretty upset. Would you like to talk about it?

There is no *one* right response to the situation in the example. There are many ways to demonstrate you are listening. You'll know your people and you'll know the details of your situation. But you can't know (i.e., assume) exactly what your staff member means. It's particularly difficult, if not dangerous, to assume you know what someone means when strong emotions like anger or resentment are involved. You

The assertive manager; direct expression balanced with responsive listening

need to check it out. In order to do that, you need to keep the dialogue open.

An angry retort or a flat denial effectively shuts down further *meaningful interaction* even though more words may be said!

In the example, any one of the responses would keep the dialogue open until you truly understood what was meant.

You demonstrate your ability to take in others' thoughts and feelings by the use of effective verbal (e.g., paraphrasing) and non-verbal (e.g., eye contact, body posture) skills.

c. THE ASSUMPTIONS

1. Something you "do," not something you "are"

Assertive skills are just that — *skills*. They are not personality traits like being inquiring, pragmatic, or enthusiastic. Assertive skills can be learned, just like decision-making, budgeting, or planning skills. What's more, practice makes you better.

Some managers are not born more assertive. If you see some managers acting more assertive than you, it's because they've learned from parents, teachers, friends, or other role models. But they had to learn, just the same.

2. Managers are people too!

You have certain rights. These rights belong to everyone, manager or not. Some of these rights include:

- The right to express your thoughts and feelings provided you don't violate the rights of others.

- The right to have your thoughts and feelings respected

- The right to make mistakes provided you accept responsibility for your actions

- The right to change your mind, to say "I don't know," or to ask for information from professionals

- The right to ask for what you want

- The right to choose when to act assertively

However, organizational life can get pretty political. A firm belief in your rights as an underlying assumption of assertive behavior will help you should you fall prey to intimidating tactics like the following:

(a) **Nullifying**: Your message is invalidated. What you remember didn't happen; what you say doesn't count. "You haven't got your facts straight, but thanks very much."

(b) **Isolating**: You are invalidated. You are forgotten or ignored. Others pretend you're not there by systematically not responding. You may even be physically or figuratively removed from the main stream of activities (meetings, memos, decisions) that affect you or your job.

(c) **Undermining**: Your future is in jeopardy. Your credibility is undermined as others create the impression that your motives, your actions, or your opinions are questionable.

You have certain rights, yes! But competent use of assertive skills will help you guarantee your rights. You'll be less intimidated because you'll be more in charge of your thoughts and feelings.

3. Choose to use assertive skills

Your right to choose when to act assertively is crucial. It deserves elaboration as a separate assumption underlying assertive behavior.

Assertive behavior is not an inherent part of your make-up — it's a skill. Therefore, you are free to choose to use the skills or not.

If you do not now use assertive skills as much as you'd like, part of the reason may be because you've been *choosing* another way of behaving. You may have been choosing to act in a passive, nonassertive way or an aggressive way for a number of reasons.

- You're not aware of assertive skills

- You're aware but you don't know how to apply assertive skills

- You act out of habit

- There's something in it for you — a payoff

Choice is a fundamental assumption of assertive behavior. Given the understanding of and the ability to apply assertive skills, such a choice leaves you actively directing your own life. With experience, you may well find that choosing to use assertive skills is more rewarding — i.e., the payoff is greater for you — than any other behavior. You can move out of old patterns and move on creatively.

Example

The manager of a small insurance office has set himself up as the one who will respond to every employee request — immediately. He feels obligated to meet their needs, demands, and expectations and to meet them on their timing. If he does not, he feels he runs the risk of jeopardizing the relationship with or the performance of his staff. He doesn't realize he's perpetuating poor performance by undermining their responsibilities.

He jumps in to help out with claim applications as soon as they ask; he locates files, he gives out phone numbers and client names that they should have on record; he drops what he's doing to listen to their comments and complaints whenever they want throughout the day.

His daily routine is clearly a series of *choices* to act nonassertively. By habit or by fear of doing otherwise — the results are the same. He finishes the day drained, distraught, distracted; he hasn't accomplished a solid block of his own work.

d. THE GOALS OF ASSERTIVE BEHAVIOR

As a manager you must make decisions, work on problems, and make judgments based on the available information, and initiate actions. You want to make the most effective decisions possible — decisions that will ensure the continued cooperation and commitment of those with whom you work.

The goals of assertive skills support your goals to build a team that works effectively together. There are two main goals.

1. Keeping the communication process going

Problems can't be solved or decisions made effectively if the information you have is inadequate or incorrect.

Boss: Why didn't you tell me you couldn't get it ready by Thursday? I could have done something.

Worker: I thought you'd be mad.

By using assertive skills, you aim to keep the dialogue open, to allow new information and honest thoughts and feelings to flow in both directions. You're now solving real problems and making decisions that stand a much better chance of being effective.

Boss: How are you doing on that report? I'm concerned about hitting the deadline Thursday.

Worker: I'm having trouble with the revisions submitted by accounting. I'd like to talk to you about the changes it will cause.

Your tone, your manner, and your words all convey the message that you and your employee are working on the same problem. You may have different sources of information, different points of view and different concerns or feelings about it, but the problem — and solving it in the most effective way — is the focus of the dialogue. You are not aiming to intimidate, to discount, to coerce, or to get what you want.

Getting what you want is *not* one of the goals of assertive behavior, contrary to some of the goodnatured ribbing that goes on when others discover you've been to an assertive skills workshop.

> Aha! So now we have to watch out, eh? You'll be wanting everything your own way around here.

Expecting to get what you want all the time will almost automatically lead you to deny others their rights and their input. You could then be prone to making decisions based on inadequate, distorted, or incorrect data. Better to keep the dialogue going until a reasonable, workable end has been achieved.

2. Building mutual respect

Respect is a key to the quality of input from others and yourself. Not respecting yourself — your own rights, needs, thoughts, feelings — or not respecting others undermines self-esteem.

A person with lowered self-esteem tends to want to protect himself or herself from further damage. This protection often takes the form of —

(a) lowered expectations (setting or accepting safe, unchallenging goals),

(b) lowered creativity (anxiety blocks innovative ideas or the desire to explore them),

(c) lowered involvement ("I don't mind what you decide."),

(d) lowered risk taking (relying on routine rules and procedures).

A person with lowered self-esteem cannot risk failure. Therefore, the safe route is the only possible route. Unfortunately, the safe route often entails squelching honest, direct expression of thoughts and feelings.

By using assertive skills you aim at nurturing and maintaining a feeling of respect between yourself and another. You give respect and expect to get respect.

Building mutual respect develops self-esteem for both of you. You are then much more likely to be making decisions and initiating actions that are both innovative and informed.

e. THE MEANS

Assertive skills depend on more than words. While your spoken message is important, research on communication has shown that the actual words account for less than 10 percent of the total message.

The rest of your message is conveyed through a variety of other channels: eye contact, facial expression, body expression, tone of voice, and so on. Chart #1 shows how you can use the various channels to convey an assertive stance.

Nonverbal communication conveys messages about such things as:

● Status — whether you feel dominant or submissive in relation to the person you are speaking to.

● Liking — the degree to which you like or don't like the other person.

● Response level — the amount of reaction the other arouses in you.

One of the defining criteria of assertive behavior is that it is honest—that is, your spoken message and unspoken message are congruent.

Albert Mehrabian and other researchers offer several critical insights concerning verbal and nonverbal communication.

First, it is difficult to manipulate or disguise nonverbal communication. Second, when the verbal and nonverbal conflict, your listener will pick up on the nonverbal message. Third, your staff and colleagues will react *negatively* to a mixed message.

Discrepancy between two channels is the chief clue that your message is not congruent. Those listening to you do two things:

(a) Take the unspoken message as the "real" message

(b) React negatively to the total message by either rejecting, ignoring, blocking, or confronting you

Eleanor praises Tom's layout while looking "through" him. Tom thinks, "She doesn't really mean the layout is good."

Philip says he is angry, but he is smiling. His employee thinks, "He can't be all that upset about it. I'm not going to pay any attention."

Next on the hierarchy of give-aways that contaminate your message are *fleeting body movements* (e.g., fluttering hands); *tone of voice* (e.g., high pitched); *body expressions in general* (e.g., slouching or leaning in); and finally, your *facial expression* (e.g., clenched jaw).

Effective integration of assertive expressions (voice tone, pacing, nonverbals, etc.) will ensure that the assertive language skills you learn will work effectively for you.

f. THE RESULTS OF ASSERTIVE BEHAVIOR

1. Real impact

The impact of assertive behavior is real. You deal with real thoughts, real feelings, and real needs to solve real problems. You focus on the present issue, present process — not inhibited by past fears or intimidated by future concerns.

2. Increased self-confidence

In the final analysis, you are the judge of your actions. Your choice to assert your rights, your thoughts, and your feelings increases your self-esteem and level of confidence. You lessen your need for others' approval. You are, therefore, less vulnerable and less insecure. You are more creative and open to risk-taking.

3. Enriched relationships

You build a base of trust and mutual respect with your coworkers. Trust is based partly on the experience of collaborating together and on the ability to manage conflict. Assertive skills contribute to both. You have the courage and competence to initiate activities and work through difficulties with others.

g. THE OTHERS: PASSIVE AND AGGRESSIVE BEHAVIOR

The fundamental differences in the message, goals, means, and results of assertive,

CHART #1
HOW TO CHANNEL YOUR ASSERTIVE SKILLS

CHANNELS	ASSERTIVE BEHAVIOR
TONE — loudness of voice and inflection	Firm, warm, well-modulated
FLUENCY — pacing of spoken word	Even pace — neither hurried nor hesitant
EYE CONTACT	Open, frank, direct, not staring
FACIAL EXPRESSION	Appropriate to the content of your message
BODY EXPRESSION — posture and hand/foot gestures	Comfortable, well-balanced, relaxed gestures
DISTANCE — from person with whom you are interacting	About one yard (metre) for normal, business-related conversations

passive, and aggressive behavior are compared in Chart #2.

1. Passive: all take — no give

Why do some managers defer their needs, suppress their thoughts, and repress their feelings?

You see some problems with the changes being put forth for the inventory control plan. You're debating with yourself whether or not to risk the disfavor of your colleagues. You think:

I better not criticize this plan. Nobody else is and it'll probably only cause a lot of hard feelings that we haven't got time to deal with.

Or your regional manager has called to change the time of the managers' meeting unexpectedly. The new time conflicts with an appointment you have with one of your key suppliers. You say:

I guess it'll be okay. I'll work something out. No, no, that's fine. Really.

CHART #2
BEHAVIOR COMPARISONS

	PASSIVE	AGGRESSIVE	ASSERTIVE
MESSAGE	You're right. It doesn't matter what I think. It doesn't matter how I feel.	I'm right. If you don't think the way I think, you're wrong. Your feelings don't count.	This is how I see the situation. This is what I think. This is what I feel.
GOAL	Avoid conflict	Get what you want — win	Communication and mutual respect
MEANS	Weak, hesitant voice	Loud haughty voice, staccato pace, demanding or sarcastic inflection	Firm, warm, well-modulated tone, even pace
EYES	Averted, look down, look away	Piercing, cold, stare down	Direct, open, frank
BODY	Slumped, slouched posture, fidgeting, wringing of hands, head-nodding excessively	Stiff, rigid, leaning-in posture, hands on hips, finger pointed, clenched hands, fist pounding	Relaxed, well-balanced posture, hands loosely at sides, relaxed gestures
RESULTS	Lowered self-respect. Pity or anger from others. Needs not met. Often feel hurt, anxious — hoping someone will guess what you want or mean. No progress on real issues.	Shaky self-respect. Must maintain control at all costs. Damaged relationships — creates hostility in others. May "gain" short-run goals at others' expense.	Maintain, build self-respect. May achieve desired goals. Work on real issues. Increase self-confidence. Develop effective relationships with others.

Why do some managers abdicate their rights to state their case and have their opinions and concerns respected, say "I don't know," or ask for clarification?

Your superior has announced a change in policy regarding the ordering of outside services. You wonder whether to state your view on it or ask why the change in procedures. You don't. You assume she knows what she's doing. You think:

> She's probably got a point there. Maybe she knows something I don't. At any rate, she must know what happened when we tried to do that before she came. I'll just go along with this.

Or, one of your employees has left in a huff because you asked him to rework a portion of last week's assessments. You feel guilty. You think:

> Maybe he's right. Maybe I am too picky. Maybe I didn't make it clear enough at first.

Why do some managers remain silent while all the time carrying on an intense inner dialogue?

One of your staff members takes over at each meeting. While her contributions are valuable, she makes it impossible for everyone else to give their views. You don't know how to stop her. You think:

> If I say anything she'll probably think I'm not interested in her ideas. If I don't say anything to slow her down, the rest of them are going to think I can't handle her.

Or, you're angry with a colleague for leaving the final wrap-up on the project in your hands, again. You think:

> If I don't say anything now, but just get this thing through somehow, I can probably…

Why do some managers never state exactly what they mean but hedge their words, ramble, hesitate, stop, or lace their comments with "you know" or "what I mean is" or "is that okay?"

> Well, what I mean is if some of the budget allocation were given to…Well, you know the groundwork we've done for it, and…what I mean is, if it were possible to…

Passive behavior is all take — taking everyone else's views and expectations on — and no give — not asserting your opinions, your needs, your rights.

The passive manager may not command much respect

17

Assertive skills let you *take in* another's feelings and opinions while you remain the judge of your response and your actions.

If you act passively, you tend to *take on* others' expectations and to *take up* their views and needs while deferring your own. You begin to feel weighed down trying to understand, act on, and meet everyone else's expectations but your own. (See Sample #1.)

In the short term, you avoid confronting and dealing with differences. In the long term, you may suffer a loss of self-respect and the respect of others; you may have your creative energy sapped by feelings of guilt and anxiety; and you may not enjoy many personally satisfying achievements.

If the benefits that result from using assertive skills increase personal and work effectiveness, then why do some managers continue to choose to act passively? Following are some of the reasons people give.

(a) Being nice

"I'm not acting nonassertively. I'm just being nice (or friendly, or polite, or considerate, or cooperative)." This is a common argument for not talking straight. It may be true, but you can check it out for yourself.

Are you receiving any silent messages from your body? "Just being polite" is a good argument as long as your own body language doesn't betray you. When you agree to a request, withhold your opinion, accept another's views, or don't ask for more information, do your palms sweat? Does your head buzz or ache? Is your stomach in knots? Are your teeth clenched?

When you are truly being considerate, your body doesn't talk back to you with all the nonverbal signals indicating conflicting messages between what you're saying and how you really feel or think.

Do you have a hidden agenda? "Just being cooperative" is a good argument as long as you are not conspiring with yourself — being passive now in anticipation that you'll receive something for it or be recognized for your cooperative spirit later.

This trap is typical of the manager who says yes to too many commitments, works overtime on a project, or defers to someone else's wishes, all the while expecting the "favor" to be returned later in the form of consideration for a promotion, extension on a deadline, unscheduled leave, a conference trip to Newport Beach.

Going to throw it back another day? "Just being considerate" is a good argument as long as you're not storing up your unspoken thoughts, your suppressed

SAMPLE #1
ASSERTIVE VS. PASSIVE

ASSERTIVE Take in	versus	**PASSIVE** Take on Take up
Demonstrated by effective listening skills. Leaves you free to choose to act or not on others' expectations.		Demonstrated by too ready acquiescence. Leaves you weighed down by others' demands and your own unmet needs.

views, your repressed feelings, and your trampled rights in an ammunition bag to hit someone with when you need extra strength.

Here's the manager who has acted as a silent accomplice for a co-worker's unscheduled absences and is now getting even:

> Remember all those times I covered for you. Well, now I want your support for...I never said anything about *you* then, even though I didn't like what you were doing.

(b) Others can't handle it

"If I were to really tell people what I think or feel, I don't think they could handle it." This is another argument for not talking straight. It has a subtle superior twist to it.

What you are suggesting with this argument is that others do not have the skills to understand and deal with your real feelings and opinions. Therefore, you must distort or withhold them. You must protect the other person.

This may be true sometimes for some people, hence the notion of appropriateness in the definition of assertive skills. This is also where the underlying assumption of choosing when to be assertive comes into play.

However, you can check yourself. Is this a legitimate argument for you to act passively? In your pattern of responses over time or with a certain person, how often do you choose *not* to use your assertive skills by telling yourself such things as:

- I don't want to hurt her.

- I don't want to get his expectations up.

- If I speak up, he'll get mad.

- I think she'd really be thrown by this news.

You are usurping the right of others to choose to use their assertive skills. By not talking straight, you deny others the opportunity to test and develop their own strengths in assertive skills. You assume their level of competency before you give them the opportunity to demonstrate it.

In effect, you take responsibility for their feelings. If someone else is hurt or disappointed or angry, you take on responsibility for that feeling.

You are not responsible for others' feelings. You are responsible for honest, direct, appropriate expression of your side, but you cannot assume responsibility for how others deal or cope with you. They are in charge of their responses.

When you become confident of your own assertive skills, you won't have to fear or anticipate the reactions of others. You'll be able to deal with them *as they happen*.

(c) Uncertain results

"If I were to really make things happen around here, I might prove to be too good (successful) or not good enough (unsuccessful)." This argument for acting passively is rarely shared with others. Acting passively can hold up real action and real progress. It can be one of the techniques used to procrastinate on decisions or actions or otherwise avoid dealing with real issues.

People procrastinate because it serves a purpose in their lives. For some, it's a way to avoid testing the illusion of their own brilliance.

This is the manager who always manages to get the project done at zero hour. When receiving praise for a job well done, the response is: "I could have done more if I'd only had another day (or week, or hour, etc.)."

Somewhere in the planning and implementation of the project, this manager uses passive tactics to ensure that there will only be just enough time to do the project but not enough time for it to be a true test of his or her abilities. What does this manager fear?

Or, this is the manager who always manages to stop just short of being "number one." Success, along with the visibility it

19

brings, induces so much guilt and/or anxiety that this manager uses passive tactics to delay, to distort, or otherwise derail a winning track record.

2. Aggressive: all give — no take

Why do some managers try to give it all — be all things to all people? They give their opinions on everything, exhort their views, think they have all the facts, all the analyses, and all the answers.

You have a deadline to meet, and a report you need from one of your staff is late. You say:

> Why isn't this ready yet? I'll tell you why it isn't ready yet. You've wasted your time on that

fool revision. You don't know how to tell those secretaries to get off their...etc., etc.

Why do some managers expect to give all the demands and to have all their demands met without question?

Some important announcements have to be made to the whole office. You want to do it when everyone is together. You say:

> I want you all here on Thursday at 2:00 for a meeting and if anybody can't make it, I don't want to know. You just be here.

Why do some managers violate the rights of others by using intimidating, dominating, overcontrolling tactics like the ones in the cartoon?

Power Plays

IT'S EITHER THIS OR THAT... WHICH IS IT?
(TAKE YOUR PICK I'M CUTTING OUT THE MIDDLE GROUND TO CONTROL THE CHOICES)

NOW LET'S BE FAIR..
(BY MY RULES)

CAN YOU PROVE THAT?
(I KNOW YOU CAN'T BUT IT'LL BE FUN WATCHING YOU TRY...)

BE SPECIFIC. GIVE ME AN EXAMPLE
(SO I CAN SHOOT IT DOWN AND PROVE YOU WRONG ON THE WHOLE SUBJECT)

BUT YOU JUST SAID... AND NOW YOU SAY
(YOU'RE REALLY ILLOGICAL DON'T YOU KNOW WHAT YOU MEAN?)

WHAT YOU REALLY MEAN IS...
(I KNOW BETTER THAN YOU WHAT YOU MEAN — SO LISTEN TO ME)

Source: 1976 © Tom Parker (Drawings) and © 1975 Theodora Wells (Balloons). From Theodora Wells, KEEPING YOUR COOL UNDER FIRE, New York: McGraw-Hill Book Co., 1980, p. 78.

Why do some managers never stop talking? They talk at their people in a terse, stacatto-paced tone all the while carrying on an intense inner dialogue with themselves.

You have to make a major presentation at a meeting with the executives. You need some audio-visual equipment, and you're worried about whether it will be working. You say:

> I thought I told you you had to be more on top of our inventory and equipment. I'm not going into this meeting unprepared. How can I count on you? Can I count on you? I've been let down before with faulty equipment and I'm not going to have that happen to me again. What are you doing about...

(Wow, am I ever uptight about this presentation. If this proposal doesn't go through...I hope they don't pressure me about...)

Aggressive behavior is all *give* — giving everyone your views and expectations — and no *take* — not taking into account their rights, needs, feelings, or opinions. The White House memo reproduced below is a good example of this.

Assertive skills let you give your views and express your feelings in ways that show equal respect for the views and feelings of others.

If you act aggressively, you will find that you land on top of others so much that they can't receive it or respond to it effectively.

White House memo covers all the bases*

Associated Press
WASHINGTON — It's not good enough, says an internal memo to aides of Charles Wick, to think of the man as director of the United States International Communications Agency. "He wants you . . . and others he meets to know that he is the close personal friend of the president."

"Do NOT argue" with Wick, the document says. "Do NOT correct him publicly."

He wants his drinks delivered promptly, expects to be passed promptly through security and doesn't like to be left standing alone at airports, receptions or meetings. And staffers should always know where "the best and fastest beauty salon" is for Mrs. Wick.

The in-house list of 25 guidelines for aides accompanying Wick on overseas trips was published Wednesday by the *Washington Post*.

The list of "Dos and Don'ts" includes:
• "Do NOT leave him standing alone, unless he requests to be left alone. At airports, receptions, meetings, keep him occupied."
• "Do NOT have security personnel at embassies or elsewhere ask him to identify himself. He expects that arrangements will have been made to have him pass through without hesitation and that the right people know who he is."
• "Do NOT pretend to know an answer. Either you know or you don't know. He wants accuracy, facts, right names and titles."
• "Do NOT smoke in his presence."
• "Do NOT let Mrs. Wick be stranded."
• "Know where he can get a haircut. For Mrs. Wick, the best and fastest beauty salon. They are both concerned about their own as well as others' appearances."
• "The director is a vigorous, fast-moving man who wants quick action. Everything should have been done yesterday. If something needs to be done, get it done right away and do not assume you will have it done later.
• For any intimidated staffers, the list ends: "Good luck."

Even some top managers expect to give all the orders and to have all their demands met.

---

*Reprinted by permission of Associated Press

The aggressive manager may be faced with hostility among the ranks

You may gain short-term success in that you'll get what you want as long as people can't defend themselves or stand up to you. But you'll feel you can never let up your vigilance. You will begin to feel thwarted at the lack of long-term commitment between yourself and your coworkers. You will feel strained and tired from exerting constant control over every situation.

Those on the receiving end will feel angry, resentful, hostile, or scared — none of which makes for rich collaborative business ventures.

Why, then, do some managers continue to choose to act aggressively? Following are some of the reasons people give.

(a) To get things done

"If I don't lay down the law, nobody will listen or do anything around here." Here's the manager who believes that the only way to get a thing done is through intimidation — make the other person afraid not to act.

Unfortunately, these attitudes and actions may be reinforced by achieving the desired results in the short term. Feeling powerless, those dominated will comply — often, however, "to the letter," and to your dismay.

Think! Think! Think about it. Couldn't you think it through for yourself! Even if I did say...You could see that...

In the long term, intimidating tactics often lead to strong undercurrents of hostile feelings among the staff or your coworkers. These feelings can erupt in more subtle ways than direct confrontation, thus sabotaging your efforts as a manager.

22

For example, you've been trying to make a tight proposal deadline for a major client. This is what you find.

Your key word processing operator just phoned in sick: "I'm sorry, I just can't make it today."

Your coworker in accounting is having trouble putting his hands on the figures used for a similar project last year: "I know they're here somewhere. I just haven't get time to look right now."

(b) It feels good

"I feel good when I sound off. It's only normal (natural) (healthy) to get mad." This argument fails to recognize the difference between describing and expressing feelings. Having feelings of anger, impatience, or anxiety are one thing. What you do with the feelings is quite another.

You are responsible for dealing with your feelings appropriately. Feelings, themselves, are not right or wrong. What you do with them can be effective or ineffective. In most cases this means that *describing* what's going on for you is more effective than expressing what's going on for you (see Chart #3).

(c) Self-protection

"I have to protect myself!" Beneath this argument lies the feeling that you need protection. Some managers use this argument when feeling vulnerable, fearing loss of control, or anticipating an attack or manipulative act from someone else. It's the old adage: the best defense is a strong offense. Your own insecurity triggers an overreaction. You lash out in an attempt to hold onto power, control, or self-esteem at all costs.

The costs, unfortunately, often include your own sense of self-respect. Acts that put down others, manipulate them, or trample their rights are rarely remembered fondly as acts to be proud of.

(d) Getting back

"They did it to me. I've got to take it out on someone." Here's the manager who goes home to "kick the cat." Acting aggressively seems justified when you've been on the receiving end of someone else's anger or domination.

Unfortunately, this whiplash effect often filters down from higher levels to lower levels as everybody "takes it out" on someone subordinate.

(e) Reaching the limit

"I'm going to show them! I've taken just about enough around here." Here's the manager who plays Dr. Jekyll and Mr. Hyde. This manager acts passively for just so long, storing up hurt, angry feelings and unmet needs. You feel justified, then, when

CHART #3
DEALING WITH FEELINGS

```
┌──────────────────────────────────────────────────────────────────┐
│  EXPRESSING                        DESCRIBING                     │
│                                                                  │
│  "You're so slow. Can't you do     "I'm getting really concerned. │
│    that any faster? You're going     I've already called the      │
│    to hold us all up!"               courier. What would help?"   │
│                                                                  │
│  "Shut up over there! How can      "I can't concentrate when      │
│    anyone think with all that        you're talking and it's      │
│    noise going on?"                  making me mad."              │
│                                                                  │
│  "You never do anything right!     "I'm getting upset with the    │
│    You don't listen."                fact that you are not        │
│                                      following the guidelines we  │
│                                      agreed on."                  │
└──────────────────────────────────────────────────────────────────┘
```

you lose your temper, often over a minor incident.

Unfortunately, those on the receiving end see your outburst as being way out of proportion to the incident. They don't know the backlog of unresolved issues you're unleashing. In their eyes, you lose a lot of respect.

You also set yourself up as someone who is unpredictable. Others are wary to work with you or to count on you.

(f) Resentment

"You've got your nerve asking me that!" Here's the manager who, for a number of reasons, finds it hard to ask favors of others or to seek information.

Perhaps, you find it hard to admit vulnerability, to have needs that others could support or fulfill, or to admit to not having everything in hand or under control.

An inability to affirm some of your very basic personal rights results in feelings of indignation, anger, or self-righteousness when others assert their rights with you.

A colleague has just asked if you and he could get together after work one day to go over some of the implications of the new tax laws that he's having trouble with. You respond:

What's the matter? Job getting too tough for you?

You may or may not agree to help, but the initial response is an aggressive response — a defensive response to protect yourself against an "intruder."

3. What triggers your defenses?

Both passive and aggressive styles of behavior are patterns of defensive responses. These responses are often triggered when you feel anxious. Anxiety can be expressed by fear/deference/withdrawal (passive) or by anger/dominance/intimidation (aggressive). Both stem from the same root — anxiety. Fight and flight are alternative ways of expressing the same problem (stress).

You choose to use passive or aggressive responses just as you could choose to use assertive skills. Your choosing may now be habit, but it is a response you learned to use and continued to use because it gave you something (protection, borrowed time, etc.)

You can, similarly, learn to use assertive skills and choose to use them as you come to value what the long-term payoff will be for you.

When you know what situations trigger anxiety for you and when you know your defensive response patterns, you can begin to change the situations or choose a different, more appropriate response.

Those who are confident of using their assertive skills feel less anxiety, thus, they do not get trapped into defensive responses.

(a) What triggers anxiety for you?

Awareness of the context that can trigger ineffective responses is the first step to being able to create more satisfying results. What "fears" underlie this anxiety? What's at stake for you? Here are some suggestions that come from others.

Which of the items below cause you the most anxiety?

- Pressure from above to do more with less

- Delegating work to others

- The creative or innovative aspects of your work

- Coordinating your work with many other people

- Evaluating the work of others

- Making public presentations

- Having your work evaluated

- Dealing with complaining or troubled employees

- Interviewing new staff

- Unrealistic deadlines

- Managing conflicts between others

- Criticizing someone's efforts

- Asking for help

In Worksheet #3, make notes for yourself to identify the types of situations which trigger anxiety for you. Are there special work situations? Are there certain people? Is it only at certain times in the week, month, year?

WORKSHEET #3
IDENTIFYING ANXIETY SITUATIONS

The following situations (people/times) create anxiety for me:

1. _____

_____

_____

_____

2. _____

_____

_____

_____

3. _____

_____

_____

(b) What is your pattern of defensive responses?

Theodora Wells, in her book *Keeping Your Cool Under Fire*, gives some clues for identifying patterns of defensiveness.

You may have learned to defer to your colleagues, clients, superiors, even your own employees. In which case, you hand over responsibility for decisions, thoughts, and feelings that rightly belongs to you. You play a "backseat" role and turn your statements into questions, silence, or self-deprecating remarks.

Or you may have learned to think of yourself as having power over others' thoughts, feelings, and needs. In which case, you act in ways to usurp their responsibility for their own actions, decisions, and feelings. You play a dominating, paternalistic role and turn your statements into demands, absolutes, or manipulative teasing.

Both patterns are defensive. They reflect many of the fight and flight responses to stress. The quiz in Worksheet #4 shows some patterns you may have observed in yourself. If you want to score yourself on these 12 types of behavior, give each item 10 points and divide the points between the passive (flight) and the aggressive (fight) columns by how often you use each behavior. For example, in the first item, if you tend to explain and justify yourself much of the time when you're defensive, you might score it seven, with only three points for how often you try to prove you're right. Total each column separately.

Use your scores to understand your own style of defensiveness better. There are no other scores to match yourself against, but there is much to be gained by becoming more aware of what it is you do when you are feeling defensive.

WORKSHEET #4
PATTERNS OF DEFENSIVENESS*

FLIGHT Passive	FIGHT Aggressive
Do you...	
____ Explain, prove, and justify your actions, ideas, or feelings more than is required for results wanted?	____ Prove that you're right? I told you so. *Now see, that proves my point.*
____ Ask why things are done the way they are, when you really want to change them? *Why don't they...?*	____ Give patient explanations but few answers? *It's always been done this way.* *We tried that before, but...*
____ Ask permission when not needed? *Is it okay with you if...?*	____ Give or deny permission? *Oh, I couldn't let you do that.*

*Theodora Wells, *Keeping Your Cool Under Fire*, New York: McGraw-Hill Book Co., 1980, p.67.

_____ Give away decisions, ideas, or power when it would be appropriate to claim them as your own?
Don't you think that...?

_____ Make decisions or take power as your natural right?
The best way to do it is...
Don't argue. Just do as I say.

_____ Apologize, feel inadequate, say I'm sorry when you're not?

_____ Prod people to get the job done?
Don't just stand there...

_____ Submit or withdraw when it's not in your best interest?
Whatever you say...

_____ Take over a situation or decision even when it's delegated; get arbitrary?
My mind is made up?

_____ Lose your cool, lash out, cry, where it's inappropriate (turning your anger toward yourself)?

_____ Lose your cool, yell, pound the desk, where it's inappropriate (turning your anger toward others)?

_____ Go blank, click off, be at a loss for words just when you want to have a ready response?
I should've said...(afterwards)

_____ Shift responsibility for something you should have taken care of yourself.
You've always done it before?
What're you all of a sudden upset for now?

_____ Use coping humor, hostile jocularity, or put yourself down when "buying time" or honest feedback would get better results?
Why don't you lay off?

_____ Use coping humor, baiting, teasing, hostile jocularity, mimicry — to keep other people off balance so you don't have to deal with them?
What's the matter, can't you take it?

_____ Use self-deprecating adjectives and reactive verbs?
I'm just a...
I'm just doing what I was told.

_____ Impress others with how many important people you know?
The other night at Bigname's party when I was talking to...

_____ Use the general you and they when I and personal names would state the situation more clearly?
They really hassle you here.

_____ Don't listen: interpret. Catch the idea of what they're saying, then list rebuttals or redefine their point?
Now what you really mean is...

_____ Smile to cover up feelings or put yourself down since you don't know what else to do and it's nice?

_____ Use verbal dominance, if necessary, to make your point. Don't let anyone interrupt what you have to say?

_____ TOTAL Passive Points

_____ TOTAL Aggressive Points

KEY FOR
WORKSHEET #2: ASSESS YOURSELF

Situation	Statement is…	One of the assertive responses would be:
1.	x(Aggressive)	Give criticism or state needs and expectations
2.	-(Passive)	Say "no"
3.	-(Passive)	State needs and expectations or give your opinion
4.	+(Assertive)	Say "no"
5.	x(Aggressive)	Give compliments
6.	-(Passive)	Say "no" or give your opinion
7.	x(Aggressive)	Give criticism or share feelings
8.	+(Assertive)	Take in criticism
9.	x(Aggressive)	Take in criticism or reflect content
10.	x(Aggressive)	Take in criticism or reflect feeling
11.	-(Passive)	State needs and expectations
12.	x or -	Share feeling
13.	-(Passive)	State needs and expectations
14.	+(Assertive)	Reflect content or feeling
15.	-(Passive)	Take in compliments
16.	x(Aggressive)	Seek information
17.	+(Assertive)	Give information
18.	-(Passive)	Give your opinion

Chapter 2 reading list

Culbert, Samuel A., and McDonough, John. *Radical Management: Power Politics and the Pursuit of Trust*. New York: The Free Press,1985.

O'Day, Rory. "Intimidation Rituals: Reactions to Reform." *Organizational Reality: Reports From the Firing Line* by Frost, Peter J., Vance F. Mitchell, and Walter R. Nord (eds.). Second edition. Illinois: Scott Forsman, 1986.

Wells, Theodora. *Keeping Your Cool Under Fire*. New York: McGraw-Hill, 1980.

3
HOW TO DO IT:
THE BASIC GIVE SKILLS OF ASSERTIVE BEHAVIOR

Sample #2 gives you an overview of the basic "give" and "take in" skills. "Give" skills will be covered in this chapter; "take in" skills in chapter 4. Each of the various skills will be addressed, giving you examples of effective statements, comments on what makes them effective, examples of ineffective statements, and opportunities for you to practice. Used together, they provide a balanced and interactive pattern of assertive skills.

Think about what it is you have to give. You have a lot of resources — knowledge, feelings, behavior. As a manager, you can use these resources to achieve long-term effective results with your team (whether they work above, below, or beside you).

You have facts and viewpoints to share, needs and feelings to express, criticism and compliments to give, and decisions to make. By using your resources in direct, honest, appropriate ways, you can make an impact on situations and other individuals that is effective in the long term.

Your aim is "clean" communication uncontaminated by guilt, anxiety, or hidden or manipulative agendas — on either side. With these basic "give" skills you can encourage cooperation, elicit action, and meet goals. This cannot be done effectively if you deny your rights or trample the rights of others. An effective manager manages resources: the communication process is a resource providing ideas, facts, feelings,

SAMPLE #2
GIVE AND TAKE IN SKILLS

GIVE	TAKE IN
1. Give information	1. Seek information
2. Give your opinion	2. Reflect content
3. State your needs	3. Reflect feelings
4. Share your feelings	4. Take in criticism
5. Give your decision: saying yes, saying no	5. Take in compliments
6. Give criticism/compliments	6. Model flexibility

needs, and behaviors to get things done. You get things done best if your resources are the best possible.

The following are examples of some of the most common give skills. These skills are one side of the total pattern of assertive skills. While these will help you meet goals, they will work much more effectively when balanced with the take in skills discussed in the next chapter.

a. GIVE INFORMATION

1. Example one

In opening a discussion with your department over bidding for projects, an aggressive or passive statement might be:

> You've got to come down in price for this client. We've got to be more competitive. How come you're out by five percent every time? If we can't do better than that, we'll all be out of here this time next year.

> or

> It's hard to pull out sub-contractors' costs in this section. I told you not to do it that way.

An assertive statement would be:

> The last two bids we put in to this client were not accepted. We were five percent higher than the winning bid each time.

> or

> When the sub-contractors' costs are added in this section, the client has a more difficult time separating the costs for each stage.

2. Example two

A coworker has stopped by your desk grumbling about how much there is left to do on the report for head office and how he's not sure he can get it there on time anyway. An aggressive or passive statement might be:

> Look, what you should do is get Blake's okay to send it in with his

regular air courier on Thursday. That will still get it in their hands by Friday morning.

> or

> Here, let's take a look. What you could do is standardize this form, run off a lot of copies, and work on those. That would save you a lot of time.

An assertive reply would be:

> There's a regular air courier to head office every Tuesday and Thursday from Blake's office at 3:00.

> or

> When Kelly did them, she used to standardize the form and run off blank ones to work on.

3. Tips for giving information

- **Be direct** — Give information as just that — straight facts, with no bias, no undertones or overtones of what you want the listener to do or not do with it. In this way, you treat others as responsible individuals who can also come to their own conclusions.

- **Be descriptive** — The more details you can include ("we were five percent higher"), the better. When statements giving information are too general ("don't do it that way"), your listener may not be sure how to interpret it and may not check with you to clarify it. A lot of time can be spent going down the wrong track if "that way" is interpreted as meaning "itemized costs" rather than "grouped costs in categories."

- **No bias** — In Example One, you've assumed a bias ("we've got to be"), implied a threat ("we'll all be out of here"), and blocked a free and full exploration of the issue. This is an opening statement. Given all the facts, from both sides of the table, you may or may not want the competitive edge with this client.

- **No advice** — The trap is jumping in too quickly to advise and moralize before you allow others to use their resources — their thinking power and their feelings about an issue. In Example Two ("what you should do"), you've usurped the other person's opportunity to think things through, use his or her own resources to analyze the situation (given the facts) and come to a conclusion.

If jumping in with advice and solutions for others is a frequent pattern for you, you may find yourself generating and perpetuating their dependence on you. This is a drain on your resources (time and energy) and a denial of their resources.

But, isn't a manager supposed to give advice, you ask? Do you mean it is never appropriate to give advice? Managers are supposed to manage the communication process to get things done with the best possible information/talent/commitment possible. Advice is appropriate, but being too quick to give advice can make the other feel stupid, resentful, or irritated.

Giving advice is appropriate but it probably won't be seen or heard as just giving advice. That's why it is not included as one of the basic give skills. When you have finished the chapters on basic skills for give and take in, you can decide whether or not giving advice still needs to be included as a separate skill.

Try Worksheet #5 to test your skills in giving information.*

WORKSHEET #5
GIVING INFORMATION

1. You've done an informal survey to find out what managers in jobs similar to yours are being paid. You discover your rate is about 15 percent lower than the industry norm. You've asked to see your superior. As you open the discussion, you say:

_____

_____

_____

2. Your bookkeeper has come to you in a dilemma because the accounts won't balance. You had discovered earlier in the day that two overdue accounts were not billed again last month. You say:

_____

_____

_____

Check your statements. Are they:
- — DIRECT
- — DESCRIPTIVE
- — WITHOUT BIAS
- — WITHOUT ADVICE

*A key to this and the following exercises is given in the appendix. But, remember, the exercises are the most helpful if you think them through and do them all yourself before checking the possible answers in the appendix.

b. GIVE YOUR OPINION OR POINT OF VIEW

1. Example one

In discussing the bidding process with your department, an aggressive or passive response might be:

> Well, I, for one, sure don't want us to spend all our time covering recalls! How could anybody think we could get away with using grade two materials?

> or

> I don't know; what do you think about putting the sub-contractors' costs in as a separate item. Do you think it might make it easier to read the proposals?

An assertive response might be:

> I'm not in favor of using grade two materials because our recall time increases too much.

> or

> I prefer to show the sub-contractors' costs as a separate item because it is easier for our clients to read the proposal.

2. Example two

Head office has asked your opinion of the monthly pricing reports. They want them retained as is, but some of the regional managers want them changed or abolished. Head office is on the phone to you. Taking an aggressive or passive stance you might say:

> I know you need the figures. I mean, I know how useful they can be. I use them myself. But, I'm sorry, don't you think it takes too much time to compile them? It's really a problem. The time, I mean.

> or

> Who said they use them? How do they want to change them? Well, I don't mind what you decide, I've got my own system under control here.

An assertive response would be:

> I agree that keeping current is vital; however, I think the time spent on them is out of proportion.

> or

> I like the format, but I don't need to have it done every month. I would find every second month just as useful.

3. Tips for giving your opinion or point of view

- **Uphold your rights** — You have a right to your opinion or point of view. Your opinion may be right or wrong, better or worse. Time and the decision-making process will tell, as the quality of the decision becomes the issue. It is not an issue whether or not you have a right to your opinion.

- **Know your view; be heard** — Be clear about your own perspective or thoughts on an issue. If you are having trouble determining what your point of view is, either seek to clarify it (using other skills) or state your present view as just that: "I can't give you a strong opinion right now. I'm having difficulty seeing what..." You do not need to have an original statement or argument in order to express your opinion. You may rephrase, repeat, or comment on what another person has said. ("I'm in favor of what Kelly has suggested...") You may agree or disagree with what others say. Or you may change the direction of the conversation. ("I think we're ignoring an important point, which is...").

- **Own it with "I"** — Give your opinion, thought, or view strength by personalizing it. ("I like the format...") Opinions couched in questions ("Do you think it might...?") or a generalized third party perspective ("How could anybody...?") lose impact.

- **No apologies** — If you have a right to your point of view, you don't need to apologize for it.

- **No intimidating tactics** — Give your view in a direct, descriptive manner. Apologies or intimidating tactics, such as too many questions (instead of stating your opinion), or drawing up sides ("Well, I, for one...") weaken the focus of your point of view. They contaminate the communication process because they generate defensiveness, frustration, or any one of a number of dysfunctional reactions in your listener.

It is much more effective to state your view clearly, sure in the knowledge that you will be able to deal with the consequences as they arise. A clear statement of how you see things keeps the communication process moving.

Try Worksheet #6 to test your skills in giving your opinion.

WORKSHEET #6
GIVING YOUR OPINION

1. Your superior is discussing your salary with you. You've presented some facts that indicate you are being underpaid compared to the industry norm. Your superior has asked you what you think you are worth. You say:

_____

_____

_____

_____

_____

2. The accountant is putting pressure on you because one of your clients is behind on the account. You don't agree with the accountant's desire to go the formal "bad debt" route because this is a well-established client whom you feel deserves more personal consideration and an opportunity to work it out. You say:

_____

_____

_____

_____

Check your statements. Do they:

— UPHOLD YOUR RIGHTS?   — GIVE NO APOLOGIES?

— INDICATE YOU KNOW YOUR VIEW?   — USE NO INTIMIDATING TACTICS?

— OWN YOUR VIEW WITH "I"?

When giving your point of view, avoid intimidating tactics

c. STATE YOUR NEEDS/ EXPECTATIONS

1. Example one

A nurse under your supervision has consistently managed her time poorly in getting the morning shift going. The student nurses are still waiting to be told what to do at 10:00 a.m.; the morning 9:00 medicine rounds still haven't been completed at 9:40, etc. You've called her in. Taking an aggressive or passive stance, you say:

> I want you to be better organized.

> or

> You're not keeping on top of things very well. The student nurses don't know what they are supposed to do and they are left standing around.

If you take an assertive stance, your response might be:

> I want you to schedule your time so that the student nurses are clear on their duties by 9:15 and the medicine rounds are finished by 9:30.

> or

> I need to be assured that the student nurses are not left unassigned later than 9:15. I want you to make this a priority.

2. Example two

The vice-president has a habit of dumping a new project on your desk with very little advance notice and little or no information regarding the content, timing, or priority. She leaves a lot to your imagination. This has caused problems in the past. The next time this happens, you take an aggressive or passive stance and say:

> I know you probably can't do it now, but can't you give me a little more information to go on? It's hard to coordinate everything around here.

> or

> Okay, sure, I guess we can fit it in. I'll just have to figure out what's involved.

If you take an assertive stance, your response might be:

> I need more details from you on the timing and priority of this project so that I can make the best use of the people in my department.

> or

> I need to know we both have the same understanding of the priority of this project. I would like to talk to you this morning about what's to be included and the timing.

3. Tips for stating your needs and expectations

- **Know what you want** — Focus clearly on what it is you want out of the situation, whether it's a request or a statement expressing your expectations. Be specific. Ask yourself: "What do I need out of this situation? As many alternatives as possible? Commitment? Fast action? Highest quality decision? Agreement on standards? When you are clearly focused on what you want out of a situation, it is very difficult for others to manipulate you or take you off on a tangent.

- **Make assumptions explicit** — Some managers make the mistake of thinking that others can accurately read their mind. They assume that "Fred must know I need those figures before the client arrives" or "Janet must realize I'm waiting for her to call before I leave." Believing that communication is unnecessary, they rely on the job description — secretary, administrative assistant, accountant, or nurse — to convey all that they expect from their employees or coworkers. "Common sense" will dictate the "proper" response expected. These managers do not take the time to make their assumptions explicit. They make statements to themselves like: "If I have to tell him what I want, that just means he doesn't know enough to be in the position."

Unfortunately, job titles, job descriptions, and even written instructions may mean different things to different people. The result is that these managers' needs and expectations are not met as anticipated, and people are left feeling angry and frustrated. So, giving others a very clear picture of your needs and expectations is critical to getting the job done and building a team that works together effectively.

When you use general terms to state your needs or expectations like "more organized" or "not on top of things," your listener may not (and often doesn't) interpret it in the way you intend. Thus, your needs still aren't met; you still may consider the other is not doing a competent job. Give your listener as many descriptive details as possible. ("Finish their duties by 9:15") Make your assumptions explicit. ("I'll be waiting for your call before I leave, Janet.") It takes more investment in the communication process on your part—more time and energy. But, compared to the time and energy often wasted later on with "I thought you meant" or "I didn't know you needed," it's one of your wisest investments.

- **Invite reactions** — State your needs as clearly and succinctly as possible. Pause. Wait for or ask for a reaction. You need to know that your request or expectation has been heard, acknowledged, accepted as is, or is about to be discussed for possible revision. Don't assume anything just because you've made your statement.

The trap here is saying too little or too much. Many managers feel stressed when they make requests or state expectations. They don't want to appear too weak or look like an ogre. Hence, they want to cut the communication process as soon as possible or control it by cutting off the listener's response and making it one-sided.

- **Do not undermine yourself**—Don't say no to yourself before you begin. If you open your statement by discounting your own needs or expectations ("I know you probably haven't," or

State your needs directly

"This is a dumb thing to ask,") you undermine the impact of your statement. Your listener is already predisposed not to grant your request or not to take your expectations seriously. If you've focused clearly on what it is you want out of a situation, it must be important to you; therefore, don't downplay its worth to you in the language you choose.

Try Worksheet #7 to test your skills in stating your needs and expectations.

d. SHARE YOUR FEELINGS

1. Example one

Your colleague has the habit of double-checking what you tell her or figures you submit.

It's beginning to get to you. Taking an aggressive or passive stance, you might say:

> Don't you trust me? I took a lot of time with that.

> or

> I think you don't trust me when you have to double-check everything.

Taking an assertive stance you say:

> I feel useless when you double-check whatever I do.

> or

> I get uptight when you can't take my word for it.

WORKSHEET #7
STATING YOUR NEEDS AND EXPECTATIONS

---

1. Your assistant has a habit of taking longer lunch and coffee breaks than scheduled. You can't rely on him to be there when you need him. You say:

_____

_____

_____

_____

2. The pricing reports have been revised by head office. You are unsure of the format now as there are several changes, which could be interpreted in different ways. You'd like to ask the accountant to take time to go over it with you. You say:

_____

_____

_____

Check your statements. Do they:
— FOCUS ON WHAT YOU WANT?   — STATE ASSUMPTIONS EXPLICITLY?
— INVITE REACTIONS?   — NOT UNDERMINE YOU?

---

2. Example two

The proposal your department recently submitted to a client was not accepted. You and your staff had all worked hard on it. You've called them together to give them the bad news. In an aggressive or passive stance, you say:

> We probably couldn't have handled it in the time they wanted anyway.

> or

> Well, you can't win them all. We'll never get in the door with that client.

Taking an assertive stance, you say:

> I'm really disappointed we didn't get it.

> or

> I feel discouraged. We all worked hard on it.

3. Tips for sharing your feelings

- **Acknowledge your feelings** — For many managers, feelings are a lost resource. They are conditioned to believe that feelings don't belong in the business world. However, your emotions are a powerful resource. By owning and sharing your feelings, you can build stronger commitment in those with whom you work. It is with the feeling component that you make contact with others and effectively engage their cooperation.

- **Own your feelings with "I feel"** — Demonstrate that you acknowledge your feelings with statements beginning with "I feel" or "I'm getting." It takes practice. After years of suppressing or ignoring feelings, you may not be sure what you feel. For example, many managers believe they are sharing their feelings when they are giving their opinion or point of view. To say either "I think" or "I feel that you do not trust me" says nothing about what you feel about not being trusted. This statement only expresses your opinion that you are not trusted. In order to discover what you feel about this, ask yourself: "If my boss did not trust me, what would I feel about it?" The answer is probably similar to the assertive statements illustrated: "I feel useless" or "I get uptight."

- **Describe your feelings** — Describing what's going on for you rather than laying it on someone demonstrates you are exercising your rights to your feelings but not denying or trampling others' rights by inducing guilt, fear, etc. In Example Two, "I feel discouraged" describes the manager's feeling and establishes the norm that it is okay to have feelings. An important role of the manager is to legitimize sharing of feelings. It is much more effective than the other response illustrated because the staff members are free, too, to acknowledge, describe, and share their feelings, and then move on to work with the situation as it really is. In the nonassertive statements illustrated, the manager first denies his feelings with a flip remark ("Well, you can't win them all,") then lays it on the group with "We'll never get..." How can staff members respond? They can't acknowledge their own disappointment in the face of that flip remark; they can *react* to the implication of "We'll never" with resentment ("We gave it our all,") or withdrawal ("Who cares?"). This is not an effective communication process from which to tackle the next problem.

- **Avoid martyrdom** — The trap with legitimizing feelings is that it is tempting for some managers to get lost in their feelings, take on the weight of the world, and use feelings manipulatively to induce pity, sympathy, recognition, and so on from others. "I guess somebody has to do it. I'm always the one. I look after so much around here." vs. "I'm annoyed that these details are left for me to do at the last minute. I'd like your help." Feelings are a rich resource, just like facts; used effectively, they keep the communication process focused on real issues.

Try Worksheet #8 to test your skills in sharing feelings.

e. GIVE YOUR DECISION: SAYING YES AND SAYING NO

1. Example one

One of your support staff has asked for Thursday off because her brother will be in town on that day. You're hitting tight deadlines and need her. Taking an aggressive or passive stance you say:

> I'm sorry, I don't think I can let you.

> or

> Yes, you can but you'd better be in early on Friday.

Taking an assertive stance you say:

> No, I'd like to let you, but I won't.

> or

> No, I won't let you have the whole day. I need to be sure the

---

WORKSHEET #8
SHARING FEELINGS

---

1. You are having a discussion with your superior concerning your performance and your salary. You've just outlined some key contributions you've made in the last six months. While doing so, your superior has frequently interrupted you to check files, answer the phone, ask questions on another matter. You don't think he's listening to you. You say:

_____

_____

_____

_____

2. Your accountant keeps asking you questions while you are working on a report. She wants to check files, verify names, ask questions, etc. You are losing your concentration. As she opens the door once again, you say:

_____

_____

_____

_____

Check your statements. Do they:

      — ACKNOWLEDGE FEELINGS?
      — PERSONALIZE WITH "I"?
      — DESCRIBE; NOT EXPRESS?
      — AVOID MARTYRDOM?

---

layout is ready. When it's ready, you may leave.

2. Example two

You have just been asked if you will take responsibility for staffing the new word processing center. You are an administrative assistant but usually Personnel handles staffing. In an aggressive or passive stance you say:

> I shouldn't do it. I mean, I'd like to but with the changeover taking so much time, and you know how much time interviewing takes...

or

Okay, if you think I can fit it in.

Taking an assertive stance you say:

> No, I won't get involved. I'm pleased with the way Personnel has handled the previous openings.

or

> I'm not sure what's involved. Are the positions to be filled from within? I'd like to think it over and tell you this afternoon.

3. Tips for giving your decision: saying yes and saying no

- **Take your stand** — Focus clearly on what you want to say: yes or no. Ambivalence will make you an easy target for manipulation. To help focus on your stand, ask yourself what you need out of the situation or what your objective is. In Example One, the manager could have had one of several different needs or objectives in mind, e.g., adherence to rules to raise standards, all hands on deck to meet a deadline, or to be seen as fair and consistent by other staff members. Each objective can have equal merit. The important thing is to be clear yourself about your objective as this makes it much easier to maintain an assertive stance in the fact of resistance.

Declare your stand with the words yes or no, accordingly. Strengthen your response by using "I will/I won't" or "I have decided to/I have decided not to." You are open to manipulative argument if you say, "I should/I shouldn't" (why not?) or "I can't" (yes, you can).

If you are uncertain about your decision, address that issue directly. Either ask for clarification or ask for time and let the other person know when you will have a decision.

- **Be brief** — Many managers feel stressed when responding to a request, especially saying no. A common reaction is to get too wordy. By acknowledging your feelings about a refusal, you defuse some of the stress. ("I'd like to let you..." or "I'm pleased with..."). However, it is not necessary to apologize for a refusal. Undue justifications and unnecessary apologies muddy the communication process.

Similarly, when saying yes, say yes unequivocally. When you tag on conditions ("But you'd better be in early Friday,") you are in danger of giving a mixed message. The unspoken message is the one your listener goes on. ("He's going to be watching me, trying to catch me. If anything goes wrong, it's going to be my fault.") If you do have concerns, state these concerns directly as a separate issue to be worked out. ("Yes, you can. I need the layout ready by 10:00 a.m. Friday, though, and I need you to do the typesetting changes. Can you do it if you come in at 8:00 a.m. on Friday?") This kind of communication process demonstrates respect for the other person's decision-making regarding his or her responsibilities.

- **Stick to it; be firm** — In the face of resistance or manipulative argument, keep coming back to your original stance. ("No, I'd like to let you, but I won't.") Just because someone is not pleased with your response (it's not what they want), doesn't mean your response is not valid. If it was truly your stand, it is still your response. You don't need a new explanation or comment each time you repeat it. If the listener still persists in arguing, you can be silent, go on to another topic, or, if appropriate, offer a compromise.

Stick to it does not mean you don't have the right to change your mind. Coming back on track with your original stand helps you deal effectively with manipulative arguing. Your response is a choice, though. Your choice can change. Just because you have always chosen to give days off in the past whenever someone requested it

doesn't mean you must continue to make the same choice. Each response is a new choice. You have the right to change your mind.

- **Don't overdose on no's** — Some managers find themselves saying no every time they talk to their employees. They are caught in an unproductive cycle in which the employees turn everything into a request to the manager. ("Can I go early?" "Can I phone now?" "May I use this?" "Can we work here?" "Will you help me?") Too many no's can squelch independent thought, induce resistance or resentment, perpetuate dependency relationships, and leave the manager feeling harried and overwhelmed.

Stick to it; be firm

There are alternatives to saying no which will help break the cycle. Several of the other skills for give and take in are effective alternatives: you can give information ("Can I go early?" "The layout is due for pickup at 12:00 p.m."); you can share your feelings ("May I use this?" "I get nervous when my reference book is used out of the office."). In this way, you encourage your employees' responsibility to think through a situation for themselves and lessen their dependency on a single word of permission from you. You feel less like an over-controlling parent and more like an effective manager.

Try Worksheet #9 to test your skills in giving your decision.

f. GIVE CRITICISM OR COMPLIMENTS

1. Example one

You like the way one of your staff handled a particularly difficult customer. An aggressive or passive response might be:

> Nobody's going to get the best of you today, are they?

WORKSHEET #9
GIVING YOUR DECISION

---

1. You and your staff had agreed on vacation schedules several months ago. Now, one of your employees wants to change his time off from June to August. The dates conflict, in part, with your vacation. You say: (Give both a yes and a no response.)

_____

_____

_____

_____

_____

2. A fellow manager in the adjoining department has fallen behind schedule on the month-end reports. She's asked you to send over two of your typists for the morning. This is not the first time you've bailed her out. You don't want to do it. You say:

_____

_____

_____

_____

Check your statements. Do they:

— DECLARE YOUR STAND?   — KEEP IT BRIEF?
— USE "YES" OR "NO" UNAMBIGUOUSLY? — KEEP IT FIRM: STICK TO IT?
                                    — AVOID A "NO" OVERDOSE?

---

or

Good for you! I wish everyone could look after our customers the way you do.

An assertive response might be:

I like the way you took the initiative with that last customer by showing him how he could make use of what he had at home with our attachments.

or

Good for you! I'm pleased with the way you took time to look for the extras that would go with that woman's suit.

2. Example Two

You don't like the way one of your staff handled a particularly difficult customer. An aggressive or passive response might be:

You'll never learn! I've told you not to offer to do a special order.

or

(a quick remark, obviously overheard by other staff) You're going to drive all our customers away with that kind of attitude.

An assertive response might be:

When you don't demonstrate an alternative model first, the customer doesn't know he may not need a special order.

or

(to an employee, alone, when the rush has slowed down) I'm concerned about the way you're waiting on some of our customers. When you answer their questions only with a curt yes or no, they have no way of knowing about our other products and services. I want you to make suggestions about…

3. Example three

During a routine staff meeting two members keep up their own low dialogue while another is giving her report. It's disturbing everyone. Taking an aggressive or passive stance you say:

Excuse me. Maybe you two could handle that when Val's finished.

or

You think this doesn't concern you down there? You'll be sorry when you find you don't have these figures later on. Now, pay attention.

Taking an assertive stance, you say:

I can't concentrate on Val's report when you two continue talking between yourselves.

or

When you don't take down the figures as they're given to you, I get annoyed at having to fill you in later. I'd like you to listen to Val's report.

4. Tips for giving criticism or compliments

Giving criticism or compliments may seem like two different, and opposite, skills. However, giving criticism or compliments effectively often depends on the same key elements. By using these key elements, the listener has a better chance of taking in either the criticism or the compliment. Criticism won't lead to future change unless it can be taken in. Similarly, compliments can't nourish and maintain effective behavior unless they, too, are understood and taken in. These tips for effective giving affect the other's ability to receive.

- **Describe behavior; give examples —** Focus clearly on the behavior that is effective (compliment) or unacceptable (criticism). Avoid the use of comparisons ("wish everyone were like you"), labels or categories ("you're unreliable, unambitious, terrific, good, etc."), or vague generalizations ("your attitude"). If you use specific examples to describe the behavior, you will be contributing to a communication process that can work between two people and have more impact on the individual and the situation. In Example Two, the employee may have a very different idea (or *no* idea at all) of what you mean by the phrase, "that kind of attitude." As a manager, if that response is your first reaction to an ineffective employee, before you speak, ask yourself, "What does that kind of attitude look like in action?" This will lead you to a more effective response describing the behavior by giving examples. The employee will have a clearer idea of what to maintain or what to change as long as no other factors are blocking his or her effective performance (see chapter 5).

- **Clarify the impact** — Offer a statement on the impact the behavior has for you or other relevant people (customers, other workers, etc.). ("I can't concentrate when you two..." or "When you answer, they have no way of knowing...") By describing the consequences, you minimize the "blaming" attitude or moralizing and implied threats often associated with criticism. ("You never listen." or "You'll be sorry.")

Clarifying the impact is important information for your listener. Information is a key resource for your employees, coworkers, etc. It provides them with the tools to manage their decisions about their behavior responsibly. In Example Three, the passive response ("Maybe you two could handle that when Val's finished.") is ineffective because it gives no information concerning the impact of their behavior. The two employees who have been interrupting may know what you mean (that you are annoyed with them for talking out of turn), but they can easily manipulate you now by responding to your "suggestion" and taking over the discussion ("No, we'll only be a minute, this is important") or by forcing a stronger reaction from you by trying to hide their inattention and continuing their private discussion by passing notes, at which point you are liable to explode with "I thought I told you to pay attention!" (Actually, you did not.)

- **Time it appropriately** — Good timing is essential for giving criticism or compliments. People tend to "close down" early when they are stressed and do not hear the words of criticism or praise no matter how effectively spoken. If your staff is under a lot of pressure, wait. Make time when the rush has slowed down to deal with problem behavior or to praise a particularly effective performance.

This may seem paradoxical since one characteristic of assertive behavior is being able to deal with things as they occur and not store them up. As a manager, you can decide about the

Time your remarks appropriately

timing by asking yourself what is the most important objective in this situation (e.g., to get this report out on time or to keep coffee cups and lunch bags off the desks; to sell as much as possible today or to build repeat clientele). If the unacceptable behavior is interfering with the key objective, deal with it. If it isn't, wait. Another clue for deciding on timing is to ask yourself, "Is this a pattern (a trend) or a one-shot occurrence?" If it is a pattern and the pattern is unacceptable, deal with it; if it's a single aberration and it doesn't usually happen, wait.

Sensitivity to timing makes good sense when you remember that one of the main objectives of assertive skills is to keep the communication process going. Timing your comment (learning when to say it) so that the other person can take it in and move on makes more effective use of assertive skills than just learning what to say.

- **Don't overload** — Most people can only take in a limited amount of criticism or praise at one time. The objective in giving criticism and compliments is to increase understanding — to feed the communication process with better information — not to make you feel relieved.

In giving criticism, decide beforehand exactly what the problem is for you. Deal only with that. Avoid bringing in old history ("and, besides, last time you never..."). If giving criticism is difficult and stressful for you and you tend to overdo it once you get started, address that issue directly. ("It's not easy for me to bring this up" or "I'm not comfortable telling you what's wrong with this report.") Sharing your feelings about the process of criticizing can often reduce the stress.

In giving compliments, decide exactly what it is that you admire or that you are pleased with. Too many compliments given too profusely can undermine your credibility and ultimately block them out for your listener.

- **Don't manipulate with compliments** — "You've got such a steady hand, how about drawing these graphs for me." This is a mixed message. Using compliments to masquerade what should be a direct request can lead to a variety of undesirable results. Your employee or coworker who's been "asked" may resent being hooked in by your tactics and blow the job just to prove you're wrong. Let your compliments stand alone.

"You've done a good job on the graphs, but I wish you'd clean up after yourself." The compliment here is used to front the criticism for the manager who has a difficult time giving criticism or stating expectations. The reinforcing effect of the compliment is lost.

"My staff don't need compliments; praise will go to their heads. They should know everything's all right unless I say something." This manager is using compliments as a scarce and coveted resource. Rather than giving credit where credit is due, he or she makes people wait for it, want it, despair for it, and, finally, withdraw from it for protection. This manager may simply be ignorant of the power of positive reinforcement, may never have had a history of compliments being given to him or her, or may be uneasy giving compliments to others.

Managers who find it difficult giving compliments may fear that praising their employees will lower the barriers; they fear making themselves more vulnerable. They may fear loss of control over their staff, thus they entrench their control by keeping a distance. They may also have been unwitting victims of others' inability to receive compliments. Too many experiences of people throwing away your compliments will eventually make you reluctant to try again.

Check your pattern of giving compliments. Is it an honest, direct, appropriate expression of your pleasure or admiration given when and where it is due?

Or, are you using compliments to mask hidden agendas that you cannot deal with directly?

Try Worksheet #10 to test your skill in giving compliments or criticism.

WORKSHEET #10
GIVING COMPLIMENTS OR CRITICISM

1. One of your employees has the habit of coming in late in the mornings. Although he often makes up the time, other staff are delayed in getting their work started because they are left waiting. You say:

_____

_____

_____

_____

_____

_____

_____

2. You are very pleased (displeased) with the way your employee has drawn some graphs for your presentation. They will (will not) reproduce clearly for overhead transparencies. You say: (Give a compliment and a criticism.)

_____

_____

_____

_____

_____

_____

_____

Check your statements. Do they:

       — DESCRIBE BEHAVIOR WITH EXAMPLES?
       — CLARIFY IMPACT FOR YOU OR OTHERS?
       — AVOID OVERLOAD?
       — AVOID MASQUERADE?

g. THE GIVE SKILLS: A SUMMARY

1. Give information

- Be direct
- Be descriptive
- Avoid bias
- Avoid advice

2. Give your opinion or point of view

- Uphold your rights
- Indicate your view
- Own it with "I"
- Avoid apologies
- Avoid intimidating tactics

3. State your needs and expectations

- Focus on what you want
- Be explicit: state assumptions
- Invite reactions
- Don't undermine

4. Share your feelings

- Acknowledge your feelings
- Personalize with "I..."
- Describe: don't express
- Avoid martyrdom

5. Give your decision: saying yes and saying no

- Declare your stand
- Use yes or no unambiguously
- Be brief
- Be firm
- Avoid a "no" overdose

6. Give criticism or compliments

- Describe behavior with examples
- Clarify impact for you or others
- Use good timing
- Avoid overload
- Avoid masquerade

Notice that there are some common characteristics running through the give skills. The skills are generally more effective when they are —

(a) focused: you are clear about what it is you want to say,

(b) descriptive: you include details and examples of the situation, your feelings, the impact, etc., and

(c) you own it with "I."

4
HOW TO DO IT: THE BASIC TAKE IN SKILLS OF ASSERTIVE BEHAVIOR

The objective of assertive skills is twofold:

(a) to keep the communication process going long enough and well enough to get the best possible information shared and understood (views, feelings, facts, etc.), and

(b) to maintain respect for both parties — self-respect and respect for each other.

An important strength of the effective manager in achieving these objectives is to demonstrate responsiveness to the other person. Your employees, coworkers, clients, and others you work with also have facts and viewpoints to share, needs and feelings to express, and criticism and compliments to give. You can greatly influence the amount and quality of information they share by your ability to take in, listen and consider, show you understand, and, when appropriate, respond by modifying your own view or behavior.

Respect and commitment on the part of those you work with are a direct result of how well you can *take in* others' views, facts, and feelings. You do not have to take on, (i.e., agree with) or take over, (i.e., become responsible for) their issues. It is the difference between debate and dialogue: "listen, then list your rebuttal vs. listen, then list their points; assume you know what they mean vs. state what you hear, then check it; overcome objections vs. respect differences."*

Your aim is clean communication uncontaminated by guilt, anxiety, hidden or manipulative agendas — on either side. With these basic take in skills you can encourage cooperation, elicit action, and meet goals. This cannot be done effectively if you trample the rights of others or deny your rights. An effective manager manages resources: the communication process is a resource providing ideas, feelings, needs, and behavior to get things done. You get things done best if your resources are the best possible.

The following are examples of some of the most common take in skills. These skills are the other side of the total pattern of assertive skills. When balanced with the give skills described earlier, they will help you meet your goals.

a. SEEK INFORMATION

1. Example one

You are working out a client's proposal with your staff. Taking an aggressive or passive stance, you ask:

> Why don't you shave five percent off the costs?
>
> or
>
> Why aren't you considering sharing these costs with marketing?

Taking an assertive stance, you ask:

> What could we do to shave five percent off the costs?
>
> or
>
> How could we consider sharing these costs with marketing?

---

*Theodora Wells, *Keeping Your Cool Under Fire.*

48

2. Example two

Your bookkeeper is having trouble balancing the accounts. He's asked for your help. In an aggressive or passive response, you might ask:

> Why do you have travel expenses here and total expenses not separated there?

> or

> Why are the expenses not separated for each salesperson?

In an assertive response you might ask:

> Where do you show the previous month's travel expenses?

> or

> Where do you show separate expenses for each salesperson?

3. Tips for seeking information

● **Do your homework** — Before you seek information, be sure you are up to date yourself on the issues concerning a situation or person. Spend some time, even a few minutes, to reflect on the background, past events, and present frame of reference of the person you are asking. When you ask questions that seem to cover old ground or that are way off base for the other person, you can be perceived as insensitive to what's going on around you. This can generate defensiveness in others ("I'd better be careful"), frustration ("Why is she asking me that now?"), or anger ("I thought we'd been over that").

● **Ask the right questions; invite data** — You are asking questions because you want others to share their feelings, contribute facts, and state their views and needs. Asking the right questions will have a great deal to do with the amount and quality of the information you receive. Ask questions that stick to one issue at a time. ("Where do you account for the previous month's...?") Ask questions that are non-evaluative. ("What could we do...?")

Who, what, where and when are fact-finding questions. How questions are best used collaboratively. ("How could we...?") Why questions imply evaluation and shut down the data-gathering process. The other person often becomes defensive and begins to respond by justifying or arguing. There is a time to evaluate, but not until all the facts, feelings, views, data, and so on are in.

Ask questions that have an answer — or at least provide a way to work out an answer. Meaningless questions or rhetorical questions demonstrate lack of responsiveness, block the communication process, and end the data-gathering phase.

Try Worksheet #11 to test your skill at seeking information.

b. REFLECT CONTENT

1. Example one

The client for a big project has just told you your proposal is not competitive and you may lose the bid. If you take an aggressive or passive stance, you might say:

> We're giving you our best prices. No one can do it for less.

Do your homework

WORKSHEET #11
SEEKING INFORMATION

1. The supplies for your department always seem to be low; standard items, such as memo pads and order forms, are sometimes not available; there was only one heavy mailing envelope left this morning. You are about to ask the clerk in charge (your employee) about it. You ask:

_____

_____

_____

2. Since the new machines were installed in production, there's been a slowdown in the schedule and an increase in rejects. You are in a meeting with your staff. You ask:

_____

_____

_____

Check your questions. Are they:
— AN INVITATION FOR DATA AND MORE INFORMATION?
— NON-EVALUATIVE?
— UP TO DATE?

or

Maybe we can change the cost structure a little.

Taking an assertive stance, you might say:

You mean our prices are too high, is that it?

or

It sounds like our timing was too long, is that the problem?

2. Example two

Your secretary has come into your office, obviously upset, but managing to keep her voice down. "I can't keep up with everything on that new word processor. No one respects the "queuing" system and they all want ev-

erything right away. I don't know how I'll get the month-end report done." An aggressive or passive response might be:

Just tell them they've all got to wait until the report's done.

or

You should be more firm when they line up things for the word processor.

An assertive reply might be:

It seems like there aren't enough controls in the system, is that it?

or

It sounds like you're having trouble getting some clout with the others, is that what you're saying?

3. Tips for reflecting content

- **Listen uncritically** — There is a time to evaluate — especially for a manager — but not before you've heard. As a manager, you need to draw conclusions, make decisions, pass judgments. However, to make the best decisions possible, you need the best resources — the best possible accumulation of facts, feelings, views, and needs. Being responsive to your employees, superiors, colleagues, and clients with an attitude of nonevaluative listening is the best way to get the information you need.

  It's very tempting to jump to conclusions prematurely, evaluating what you've heard (or what you think you've heard) in terms of good/bad or right/wrong. The manager's ineffective response in Example One ("Maybe we can change...") illustrates a common trap of wanting to jump in with decisions and solutions before understanding what was meant. In this example, the manager assumes the client is wrong, or that the situation can be corrected, before she clarifies what the client meant. The way to listen uncritically — to stop yourself from evaluating too early and jumping in with decisions and solutions — is to demonstrate you have been listening by reflecting back what you've heard.

- **Interpret meaning** — Appropriate body language demonstrates you are listening. Eye contact, relaxed posture, a thoughtful facial expression, standing still, not making impatient gestures like finger tapping are all important. To make the most of the communication process, however, you need to demonstrate what you've heard — before you act on it. This assures the other person that his or her views, information, feelings, and needs have been taken into consideration. Even if the ultimate decision or action is not what the speaker desired, having been heard makes the decision more acceptable.

  The best way to demonstrate you've heard the other person is to reflect back the content of the statement in your own words. Because it's your interpretation of what you've heard, there can be many different responses to the same statement. In Example Two, two different, but equally valid and equally responsive, statements are illustrated. There could easily be other interpretations as well. Two others might be: "I imagine you're having a tough time feeling as competent on this new model as you used to, aren't you?" or

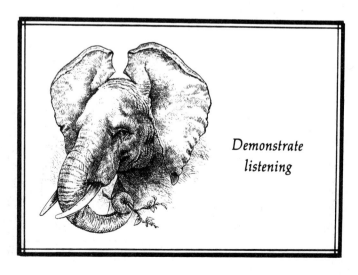

Demonstrate listening

"Do you mean you need some temp help for the month-end report?"

The manager who acts on any interpretation before checking it out is headed for trouble. The result will be time wasted in wrong actions and unmotivated employees who feel misunderstood.

Use your own words to reflect back the content. Simply parroting back the exact words the other has said ("You can't keep up with everything, is that it?") generates annoyance and blocked communication. Your employee will feel patronized.

Notice that an effective paraphrase, or reflection of how you interpret another's statement, implies tentativeness. You cannot be sure your interpretation is correct until the other person responds with something like: "Yes, that's it!" The aim of paraphrasing is to keep checking out your interpretation until both you and the speaker are on the same wave length. Until you are both on the same wave length, it's premature for you to evaluate, criticize, or advise. All the facts aren't in.

Some common introductory phrases that convey tentativeness include:

> It sounds like...
> Do you mean...
> So...
> I guess...
> In other words...
> You think...
> So, you're saying...

Some common checking out statements include:

> Is that right?
> Is that it?
> Is that true?
> Is that what you mean?
> Is that what you're saying?

These phrases, used at the beginning and at the end of your interpretation, allow the other person to come back with a clarifying comment ("No, I don't think I need any temp help, but I am having trouble keeping other hands off the prioritizing of the projects.") You demonstrate your responsiveness by reflecting content, not reacting to it. Both views are respected, and you are on your way to solving the real problem.

Taking time to reflect back the content of what you hear slows down the almost instinctive impulse you may have to take on responsibilities that rightly belong to the speaker or to take up issues that aren't justifiably yours.

Being responsive does not mean being responsible for everything and everybody. Being responsive to your workers, colleagues, and clients by demonstrating listening lets the responsibility for what they feel and think remain on their side.

Try Worksheet #12 to test your skill at reflecting content.

c. REFLECT FEELINGS

1. Example one

One of your employees has had a particularly bad run-in with a client: "Then he said to me, 'If you can't give me better service than that, you shouldn't even be working here.' And I was the one who tried to push that special order through for him! I'm through with going out of my way." Taking an aggressive or passive stance, you respond:

> Come on, John. We've all got to learn to roll with the tough ones. Let's get on with it.

or

> Well, next time you should check with Customer Services first.

Taking an assertive stance, you respond:

> Boy, you really feel unappreciated, don't you?

or

WORKSHEET #12
REFLECTING CONTENT

1. The accountant has approached you about one of your clients who is behind on the account. "I don't see how we can carry this guy any longer. It's hard enough having to keep all the current accounts in order without having to drag along old history and keep track of that as well." You respond: (Write two different paraphrases to reflect two different interpretations of the content.)

_____

_____

_____

_____

_____

_____

_____

2. Your office supervisor has come to you complaining that she's getting orders from the department manager (your superior) that contradict what you've told her. She says, "It makes life too confusing around here to do one thing for one person and have to change it the next day. How can I get anything done? It makes me look like a fool." You respond: (Write two different paraphrases to reflect two different interpretations of the content.)

_____

_____

_____

_____

_____

_____

_____

Check your responses. Do they:
- — INDICATE THAT YOU LISTENED UNCRITICALLY?
- — DESCRIBE YOUR INTERPRETATION?
- — SHOW TENTATIVENESS?
- — INDICATE YOU ARE TAKING TIME?
- — INDICATE YOU ARE NOT TAKING ON SOMEONE ELSE'S RESPONSIBILITY?

It's pretty discouraging when no matter what you do, you can't please someone.

2. Example two

Your administrative assistant has started a discussion with you about her career: "I've been here three years now and I'm still doing the same thing. I know it inside out. I thought I'd be able to learn a bit about the rep's job but somehow that hasn't happened. I don't know what's next." An aggressive or passive response might be:

> You've got a good job here. You do it well. You've got nothing to worry about.

or

> Everybody wants to go faster than they do. That's normal.

An assertive response might be:

> Seems like you're feeling disappointed with your progress so far.

or

> Hmm…You're feeling pretty shaky about the future, is that it?

3. Tips for reflecting feelings

- **Acknowledge feelings** — The first priority for anyone speaking to you with an emotional overtone is to be heard — to have his or her feelings understood. The key to showing empathy (understanding of the other's feelings) is acknowledgment. This is not agreement or disagreement, nor a solution for the problem, nor a decision, action, nor a piece of advice. It is just hearing the person.

  When an employee (or anyone with whom you work) is feeling hostile, discouraged, or confused, you don't have to decide if he or she is right to feel that way. You also don't have to do anything about it unless you choose to later. The trap is denying others' feelings because you feel responsible for doing something about them. You think you have to make sure everything is okay and solve everyone's problems. Instead, demonstrate your ability to take in, without taking over, by giving your employee an opportunity to talk it through. This leaves the person who has the feelings in charge of what to do with the feelings, while it still gives you the information you need. Often, simply being heard and having feelings acknowledged resolves the situation for the other person.

  It helps to make a distinction between having feelings and what you do with feelings. You can acknowledge an employee's frustration over a difficult client, without evaluating it, but you can, and should, disagree with the action when the employee takes out his or her frustration by ignoring the client's order.

- **Interpret emotional tone and label** — Use your own words to interpret the emotional tone you've heard and give the feelings a label (unappreciated, disappointed, shaky). When you rely on a general statement such as: "I understand how you must feel," neither you nor your employee will be clear on what it is you understand. As a result, you do not demonstrate responsiveness; your employee feels frustrated as well as mad, discouraged, or whatever the initial feeling was; and the communication process has nowhere to go except to dissolve into a jousting match. ("No, you don't." "Yes, I do. I said I understood, didn't I?" "But…" "Listen, what more do you want?")

  When you reflect how you understand the emotional tone ("You're feeling pretty shaky about whether you can count on anything in the future, is that it?"), your employee can agree ("Yes, things are suggested to me, but nothing different really happens") or disagree with your interpretation ("No, it's not that really. I'm more mad at myself for letting things slide. I don't really know how to start

on those suggestions you gave me").
Now the two of you have something
to work with.

- **No tricks to evade acknowledging feelings** — Managers operate under tremendous time pressures. This often serves to reinforce the belief that "I can't afford feelings around here." However, the tricks used to evade acknowledging others' feelings are often very costly in terms of lost resources. When you deny or discount feelings, you stand to lose out on the real information you need. When you give unwarranted advice, you often have to backtrack later, using up valuable time, to redirect misguided efforts. When you submit others' feelings to pop psychology or philosophizing, you may undermine needed motivation. In all cases, you lose out on developing the competencies in those with whom you work which would make them better able to deal with their feelings, express them, and maintain self-responsibility for their actions.

    Taking in feelings effectively makes the best use of present resources (information, feelings, attitudes, facts) and builds future resources in terms of increased confidence in personal abilities — yours and others.

Try Worksheet #13 to test your skill in reflecting feelings.

d. TAKE IN CRITICISM

1. Example one

The client for a big project has just told you your proposal is not competitive and you may lose the bid. An aggressive or passive response might be:

> Sure, we're competitive. We're giving you our best prices.

> or

> I don't know where you're going to do any better than that. Do you know what maintenance costs are these days?

An assertive response might be:

> What is it about the proposal that's shooting it down?

> or

> You're right. We blew it on our estimates for maintenance costs.

2. Example two

A colleague is reporting back to you on your presentation to the board earlier this morning: "Damn it, Mary, no one could understand what you were talking about this morning!" Taking an aggressive or passive stance, you respond:

> Oh yeah. Well, if you'd paid more attention, I guess you could have understood.

> or

> I didn't see you up there, did I?

An assertive stance might be:

> What was it about the way I spoke that made it hard to understand?

> or

> You're right. I've got a lot on my mind right now and couldn't focus.

3. Tips for taking in criticism

- **Explore it; don't react** — If the criticism is relevant to your functioning as a competent, effective manager, you need it. You need all you can get in a usable form. Most of us have conditioned ourselves to react to someone's evaluation of us or our actions with denial or counter-attack. This may give you temporary relief, but it does not contribute anything to the resources (facts, feelings, information, attitudes) you have to work with.

    To make the most of others' views, encourage a full exploration of the issue their criticism raises. Ask non-threatening, probing questions. Questions that focus on the issue or on you, not on the critic, are more effective. "What is it about?" is better than "Why do you say

WORKSHEET #13
REFLECTING FEELINGS

1. Your production supervisor has been telling you about his troubles with the new machines: "The trouble is our old orders still need the old format and the new machines won't do that unless we run it through twice. No one knows what's involved and I'm getting it because we're behind. But we're going as fast as we can." You respond: (Give two different interpretations of his feelings.)

_____

_____

_____

_____

_____

_____

_____

2. A fellow manager is having difficulty keeping trained staff in her department. Over coffee, she complains to you: "At our rates, I can't keep them once we've trained them. I haven't even got people good enough to do the training now. I'm sick of trying to do a good job with half of what I need to do it." (Give two different interpretations of her feelings.)

_____

_____

_____

_____

_____

_____

_____

Check your responses. Do they:
- —ACKNOWLEDGE OTHERS' FEELINGS?
- —AVOID AGREEING OR DISAGREEING?
- —REFLECT AND LABEL FEELINGS?
- —AVOID USING TRICKS TO EVADE ACKNOWLEDGMENT?

that?" "How could I...?" is better than "What would you do?"

Ask for examples, not to test the critic, but to clarify your understanding of the issue: "I'm concerned about my presentation. What do I do in the presentation that doesn't seem to work well?" The answer may be as simple as, "Well, when you're finished with the overhead, you don't switch it off. Even though you're talking about something else, the other chart's still up there." Now you understand!

- **Seek suggestions** — It is very legitimate, once you've explored the criticism, to ask for alternatives and seek suggestions. Others have valuable insight into how you could be more effective and have more impact. If you are responsive to it, you can benefit. The danger is to cut the communication process too soon, once you've discussed the criticism. You're probably feeling good. ("Did we ever work that one through and look at what I've found out.") Your critic is feeling good, too, having made a significant contribution. ("Gee, she actually listened and we were able to work it through.") It's an excellent time to move into a discussion of what to do differently next time: "How could we recoup on this proposal?" Or, in the case of the employee who complained that you never listen to any of the staff's ideas: "Would you like to try a regular informal half-hour rap session each Friday morning? Would that work better?"

- **Own your mistakes** — When you are criticized for a mistake you did make, own it. Admit your errors clearly and unambiguously. ("You're right." "I blew it.") It's not the foul-up, but the recovery that counts. Avoid long-winded justifications. Remember, you have the right to make mistakes provided you accept responsibility for the consequences. Move on to deal with the consequences in a positive, creative way. "I'm concerned that the rest of the board may feel the same way. I could give you a written copy. Would that help?"

- **Ignore it, don't buy into manipulation** — Ignoring someone's input may not seem responsive at first. However, when you are faced with manipulative criticism, you need to deal with it in a way that maintains your self-respect and does not discount the other person. Baiting remarks ("Bet you're not going to be ready with that report by Friday"), sarcasm ("Look who's making a big speech"), and hostile or irrelevant remarks can trap you. When the criticism is not relevant — that is, you don't need to explore it in order to get better information — ignore it. Let it roll off you, unchallenged. You can do this by agreeing in a general way: "Yeah, some might think so" or "It must seem like that." Or, you can remain silent.

The trap is becoming hooked into someone else's game. Then you are not demonstrating responsiveness. You react; you are no longer in control of choosing how you want to act. Faced with manipulative criticism, take in the comment without taking up the challenge. Taking up the challenge uses up your resources and contributes nothing useful to the process.

Try Worksheet #14 to test your skill in taking in criticism.

e. TAKE IN COMPLIMENTS

1. Example one

The vice president has called to tell you what a great job you did on getting the new inventory control system in place. An aggressive or passive response might be:

> It's still not perfect. There are a few things I've got to work out yet.

> or

> Well, it sure was a lot of work. We had to have a weekend staff in there to clean it up, you know.

WORKSHEET #14
TAKING IN CRITICISM

1. Your production supervisor has come to see you about the delivery dates you arranged for a big order next week. She says, "You've really got us in trouble with that deadline." You respond:

_____

_____

_____

_____

2. A colleague stops by your office after the manager's meeting and comments on the fact that you got your plan for new staff approved. "I don't know how you pushed it through in that state. You must have pull." You respond: (Give one response to explore the criticism and one response to ignore it.)

_____

_____

_____

_____

Check your responses. Do they:

      — EXPLORE IT, NOT REACT TO IT?
      — ASK FOR EXAMPLES?
      — SEEK SUGGESTIONS?
      — OWN YOUR MISTAKES?
      — IGNORE IT, NOT CHALLENGE THE IRRELEVANT?

An assertive response might be:

> Thank you. I'm pleased with how it's running, too. One of the changes I'm planning is ...

> or

> Thank you. I'm glad you called to tell me.

2. Example two

A colleague is reporting back to you on your presentation to the board earlier this morning: "Hey, Lee, that was an excellent presentation. I found it really useful." An aggressive or passive response from you might be:

> Oh, it wasn't anything.

> or

> Thanks, your speech was super, too.

An assertive response might be:

> Thanks. I felt good about it, too.

> or

> Thanks, I'm glad you could use it.

3. Tips for taking in compliments

● **Soak it up** — Learn to let a compliment soak in; let it sink right down to the place where you know it's true.

With your first response, acknowledge the compliment. People do this nonverbally when their eyes shine, they make good eye contact, and smile, or verbally when they say, "Thank you. I'm glad you called to tell me." An unacknowledged, unappreciated compliment is a lost resource.

Many managers can dish out praise easier than they can take it in. Some aren't sure how to appear modest while still showing appreciation; some don't like feeling beholden, therefore, won't allow others to give them anything; some suspect ulterior motives; others expect criticism to follow on the heels of commendation; and others fear they'll be expected to keep up the good work and may not be able to. Yet compliments are a valuable resource given to you. They help maintain and build self-esteem. Higher self-esteem, in turn, can lead to further creativity and competency (see chapter 2).

Listen to the words and the emotional tone in the same way you would listen to other statements. Learn to let it in and, if necessary, ask for clarification or examples. ("Which part of the presentation was most helpful to you?") Share your feelings about the issue or situation, too, if that's appropriate. ("I felt good about it, too.")

Your ability to be responsive benefits you. But it is also critical for the speaker, the one who is giving you compliments or praise. Don't deny real contributions to the communication process. Remember, it's a resource. Effective working relationships depend on both parties being able to exchange appreciation and respect. When you block others' compliments to you, you undermine the relationship and the process. Too many responses that discount others' compliments to you may eventually result in no more being offered. The result is scarcer resources and a message from you to the speaker that says: "Your views don't count."

- **Don't scramble to return the compliment** — Let the compliment given to you stand alone. The rush to reciprocate with another compliment interferes with your ability to let it soak in. You are too busy desperately casting around for something to say in return.

Sometimes, a returned compliment may be in order, after you acknowledge and show appreciation for the one given you. But, you are not obligated. If you feel obligated, you are reacting, not being responsive.

Try Worksheet #15 to test your skill in taking in compliments.

f. MODEL FLEXIBILITY

1. Example one

Since you and your production supervisor have been able to discuss the difficulties in meeting schedules with the new machines, you now understand the situation. Taking an aggressive or passive stance, you say:

Soak up compliments

Okay, I guess you're right. Anyway, I've got too much going on right now to think about it any more. Go ahead.

or

I still think I'm right but I haven't got time to prove it to you, so go ahead.

Taking an assertive stance, you say:

I can see where I've been out of whack in estimating the time for the old orders. I'll check with you first until those orders don't come in any more.

or

I'm really pleased with how quickly we worked this through by getting together. I'm glad you suggested it. Let's continue meeting like this once a week instead of using the memos I used to write.

2. Example two

Your bookkeeper has been working out a better way to handle the time sheets. You've

WORKSHEET #15
TAKING IN COMPLIMENTS

1. Your administrative assistant has come back to talk to you a week after you and she had a particularly lengthy discussion about her career. She says, "I really appreciate the time you took with me last week. Your questions were really helpful in getting me to think more clearly about where I want to go." You respond:

_____

_____

_____

_____

_____

2. A customer has called you to say how pleased she was with the way you handled her recent mortgage application. You respond:

_____

_____

_____

_____

_____

Check your responses. Do they:

— SOAK IT UP?
— ACKNOWLEDGE?
— AVOID THE SCRAMBLE TO RECIPROCATE?

had several discussions. He's now come in with what looks like a better system. An aggressive or passive response might be:

> Oh, yeah, well, that's what I said. Remember? Or at least that's what I was thinking about, too.

> or

> I guess you should have been doing it like that sooner.

An assertive response might be:

> I was wrong. I didn't think of that. I can see now why it's better to keep the travel time separate for each salesperson's trip.

> or

> That's much more straightforward. I didn't think of it. I can easily make sure you get the information you need to do it each month.

3. Tips for modeling flexibility

- **Adapt your behavior; modify your view** — The communication process is a resource to get things done. When you think of it like that, it's easier to let go of your views or change your behavior in order to be more effective in reaching goals. Use the communication process as a resource. Manage it. Fine tune it with the give and take in skills until you have the best possible information, sharing of feelings, and statements of needs and expectations — yours and others'.

  As a manager, you play a key role in modeling flexibility. Not only will you be contributing to a better resource yourself, but others will follow your lead. If you can adapt your behavior and modify your view in response to better information, your staff and others you work with will also feel freer to change their views and behavior as needed.

- **Share the glory** — Come out of the closet with your responsiveness. When you do change your ways and your views as a result of others' input, let those who are responsible for it

know about it. ("I'm glad you suggested it. Let's continue meeting.")

You lose the positive impact your responsiveness can have on your working relationships when you discount the other's efforts or when you usurp the credit. Your staff is less likely to continue to contribute in the same way if you must take all the credit for the progress or changes.

Try Worksheet #16 to test your skill in modeling flexibility.

g. THE TAKE IN SKILLS: A SUMMARY

1. Seek information

- Do your homework
- Invite data
- Don't evaluate

2. Reflect content

- Listen uncritically
- Interpret meaning
- Be tentative
- Take time; don't take on responsibility

3. Reflect feelings

- Acknowledge others' feelings
- Don't agree or disagree
- Reflect feelings and label
- Avoid tricks to evade acknowledgment

4. Take in criticism

- Explore it; don't react
- Ask for examples
- Seek suggestions
- Own your mistakes
- Ignore it; don't challenge the irrelevant

5. Take in compliments

- Soak it up
- Acknowledge
- Don't scramble to reciprocate

WORKSHEET #16
MODELING FLEXIBILITY

1. Head office has sent you a revised system for the pricing reports. It will be a more effective system for you in the long run because it can be done quicker and read easier by field staff. However, adopting it means giving up your view that it should be categorized by client, not product. H.O. is on the phone. You say:

_____

_____

_____

_____

_____

2. You've always thought that career planning should be the responsibility of individual employees and, maybe, Personnel. You do performance reviews on present jobs. Now, however, you've learned from a recent workshop how career development and performance reviews work together. You're planning to change the way you handle these discussions with your staff so that they are more a part of total career planning. This seems to fit better as well with some of the comments and requests you've been getting from your staff. During the staff meeting this morning, you tell them:

_____

_____

_____

_____

_____

Check your responses. Did you:
— ADAPT YOUR BEHAVIOR?
— MODIFY YOUR VIEW?
— FOCUS ON RESOURCES?
— SHARE THE GLORY?

6. Model flexibility

- Adapt your behavior
- Modify your view
- Focus on resources
- Share the glory

Notice that there are some common characteristics running through the take in skills. They are generally more effective when they —

(a) acknowledge others' views, facts, feelings, and needs, and

(b) are used without evaluation; you respond without jumping to conclusions, taking over to make decisions, or taking on issues before both parties agree on the interpretation.

5
HOW TO HANDLE THE POOR PERFORMER*

A problem employee who performs poorly over the long term drains you and your department of valuable resources: time, energy, and a constructive contribution of information, feelings, views, and needs, not to mention the obvious loss of productivity. This often results in you or your department not achieving goals and not building working relationships you can count on for commitment and innovation.

a. OVERCOME THE RELUCTANCE TO DEAL WITH IT

Often managers are reluctant to deal with an employee whose performance is unacceptable. They justify it in a number of ways: "I'm stuck with him. He'll never change." "No one called it before, so how can I start now?" "I haven't got time to deal with it." Ask yourself who you are doing it for.

The script in Worksheet #17 shows how performance problems are often handled ineffectively because of time pressures, habit, or lack of a command of style. As you read it, note beside it all the mistakes you can find.

Check your list of mistakes with the ones described below:

(a) Blaming: aggressive, accusing style; manager evaluates employee's behavior before all the facts are in; focusing on the person ("You really put me...") not the problem;

Overcome your reluctance to deal with it

---

*The ideas and dialogue in this chapter were originally developed for video training tapes with Professor Peter Frost of the Faculty of Commerce, University of British Columbia, Vancouver, Canada.

The manager has just called the clerk, Kelly, into her office. This is the first discussion the manager has had with the employee concerning the problem.

		The mistakes
Clerk:	Good morning. What's up?	
Manager:	Hi, Kelly. Take a seat. I've just come back from a meeting and I want to get some things straightened out right away. You really put me in an embarrassing position this morning and it wasn't the first time. I have just come back from an important meeting with a number of key managers. I needed copies of the manpower report for our discussions on the manpower planning program. You're supposed to keep them on your shelf. They weren't there. I needed blank tapes to record the meeting. There was only one memo pad. I needed pads for everybody. And yesterday, my secretary told me that there's no letterhead and brochures for the mail-out we're doing for the programs. What's the problem? You should have them.	
Clerk:	Well, the tapes were there last night. The reports were there last night. Other people come through there. I can't keep on top of it if other people are going to go in there and take things.	
Manager:	Kelly, who's in charge of the department? You're in charge, that's who. This is not the first time. It used to work very well. Now, this is at least the fourth time I can recall in the last couple of months that we have been short on supplies of tapes and brochures.	
Clerk:	But, nobody listens to me. And, besides, we only have so few. I know I'm supposed to call the suppliers and keep a backlog, but...	
Manager:	Why don't you do it?	
Clerk:	I do. They just don't listen and they don't send them and I don't have enough money to get enough.	
Manager:	You've got to show them who's boss around here.	

		The mistakes
Clerk:	I do, but they don't listen. And people just come in and help themselves. I can't be there and do other things. I helped you with that training package. You asked me to take some extra time to do that. I took my lunch hours. I can't work on that and also watch the supplies.	
Manager:	Well, you know I appreciate you doing that, but, it shouldn't get in the way of your normal work. As far as I am concerned, we told people you were in charge of the department's supplies. You should be able to look after your own area. Now, I am not prepared to have that happen again. I was there yesterday, too. Everything's a mess. You could be a little more tidy, you know.	
Clerk:	I'm not the only one that goes in there. People just do what they used to do. They don't listen to me.	
Manager:	You must straighten them out. As far as I'm concerned that is your job and I have a lot of other things to do here. I can't be chasing after things like this. It should be automatic for me. I don't want to have to deal with it again. You take care of it. And that's all for now.	
Clerk:	Okay.	

(b) No request for employee's viewpoint: manager assumes she knows all the facts and all the answers;

(c) No listening: manager doesn't reflect or explore content when employee tries to contribute; not sensitive to employee's feelings of frustration and disappointment;

(d) No support: manager doesn't offer views, information, or decisions to give assistance;

(e) Ambiguous expectations: manager makes general demands ("You've got to show them.");

(f) No recognition: employee's effective contributions are discounted ("It shouldn't get in the way.");

(g) No closure: manager doesn't check that both have the same interpretation of what actions each will take, by when, and when they'll get together again. ("You take care of it.").

b. THE SYSTEMS VS. COMPETENCY APPROACH

There are two basic approaches to performance problems the first time you address the problem. You can call it a competency issue, meaning that, like the manager in the script above, you conclude that the person is the problem; he or she is incompetent and either cannot or will not do the job adequately. Or, you can call it a systems issue, meaning that you focus on the problem, not the person, and explore, with the employee involved, the obstacles to be overcome and actions to be taken. Before concluding that the employee is incompetent, you exhaust all other possibilities that could be blocking the employee from performing well.

The results from the two approaches are dramatically different.

1. The competency approach

The script in Worksheet #17 illustrates the competency approach. What are the consequences of using this approach? In this case, the employee probably feels inadequate, questions her own abilities, and loses confidence.

To protect herself from any further attacks to her self-esteem, she may counterattack, withdraw, or play it safe in the future. She won't take the initiative for fear of making a mistake, nor contribute views or information for fear of being discounted.

The hostility generated may surface at the most inopportune times for you, the manager. Many employees whose rights have been trampled and whose views, feelings, and needs have been discounted cannot confront the source of their anger (you) directly. Instead, it may show up in other ways: being unable to find an important file for you when your client is waiting in your office; phoning in sick when you're trying to make a deadline; turning off customers with an indifferent attitude; quitting without giving notice.

One of the traps of an aggressive behavior style is the short-term relief (reward to you) of blowing off steam.

Later reflections on blowing off steam lower a manager's self-image. It can lead to the manager questioning his or her ability to handle situations effectively. Self-doubt undermines confidence.

As working relationships with the staff deteriorate, the manager can't count on cooperation and support. Fear of losing control increases anxiety.

By not exploring the problem or offering assistance, the manager may be liable for accusations of wrongful dismissal or unfair disciplinary practices later.

By taking a competency approach, the manager has not reached an agreement with the employee on what the problem is.

There are also consequences for the rest of the staff. Rumors travel. Laying blame sets an unhealthy norm. Other employees learn that whenever anything goes wrong, they'll be blamed personally. They soon adopt a "cover yourself" attitude. They won't take any chances on being caught; they won't take risks; they won't be innovative, creative, or take initiative. They won't contribute anything except the absolutely essential requirements of the job.

A hostile employee who can't confront you directly may decide to take it out on you indirectly by going to the union, if there is one. An increase in the number of grievances, warranted or not, takes your time and energy away from achieving your goals. In addition, the adversarial stance between union and management is strengthened — with the union gaining clout.

In addition, unhappy, frustrated, angry employees do not make positive remarks to friends and the general public. Union and disciplinary issues can become hot media topics. The organization's image in the community may be at stake.

By focusing on the person with accusations, implied or otherwise, of incompetency, the manager has blocked any real exploration of the problem. Thus no new information is revealed. The employee and the manager are not working on a common objective.

A manager may not know what the real problem is

Even if the manager does state some facts and lay down expectations, the employee is likely to shut down under stress and not hear them. Superficial or temporary adjustments may be attempted, but the real problem still exists.

2. The systems approach

The list of negative consequences described above is imposing. Many, if not all, of them are common and quite possible as a result of taking the competency approach to performance problems. All those consequences use your resources in ineffective ways. In addition, a major problem with all of the consequences is the time needed to sort things out later. Is it better to invest time now or later? Is it better to deal responsibly with a problem when it occurs so that it doesn't ferment or is it better to spend time cleaning up the spillover later when it affects your department, union, and organization as a whole.

One of the basic rights that assertive behavior affirms is your freedom to choose. Even if you have a long history of ineffectively handling performance problems, you have the right to now choose to act differently — more responsibly and more effectively.

You can use the basic give and take in assertive skills to deal with the poor performer in a systematic way. Consider Sample #3, a replay of the previous script. The manager now chooses to approach the problem from a systems view, focusing on the problem, not the person, and together they explore the obstacles in the system. As you read Sample #3, note the assertive skills used and the results.

By using the systems approach to explore a problem with an employee, you can expect some, or all, of the following consequences.

The employee will have increased self-esteem; positive feelings of confidence in self and support from manager; willingness to contribute facts, views, needs, and feelings; willingness to take initiative and risks; and practice in developing skills in communication, analysis, and decision making.

The manager will maintain or increase self-esteem; improve skills in communication and developing staff; develop working relationships based on commitment and innovation; gain information needed to achieve goals; and gather systematic documented evidence should future disciplinary action be necessary.

In addition, new information will be revealed about the problem. There will be a shared understanding of the issues and a common objective. And, perhaps, the *real* problem will be solved.

Try the systems approach *first* — in the first discussion concerning the problem

HANDLING PERFORMANCE PROBLEMS — THE SYSTEMS APPROACH

The manager has just called the clerk, Kelly, into her office. This is the first discussion the manager has had with the employee concerning this problem.

		Skills and results
Clerk:	Good morning. What's up?	
Manager:	Hi, Kelly. Take a seat. There's a problem I'd like to discuss with you. I've just come back from a meeting with a number of senior managers in our manpower planning group and I was faced with a really difficult situation. I felt embarrassed because I couldn't bring the equipment and supplies we needed. I needed memo pads and tapes so we could record it. There weren't enough on the shelves. I needed copies of the manpower report and they were missing. This is not the first time this has happened. I wondered if you could tell me a little bit about what you see as the problem.	Give information; describe Share feelings; describe use "I" State needs Seek information
Clerk:	I am having a problem with that. So many other people just help themselves to the supplies and I find that, unless I am right there, I can't keep on top of it. I'm in two rooms, you know, and in one room I'm doing my other work and the supplies are in those storage rooms. I know I'm responsible, but people just help themselves.	Result: not so defensive, willing to give information
Manager:	You sound pretty frustrated with the way the work is set up at the moment. The problem I have is that I can't afford to be caught short. Do you have any ideas? Any sorts of things we could do to solve the problem? I need to be able to count on adequate supplies all the time.	Reflect feelings and label State needs Seek information State needs; focus on what you want
Clerk:	I know. I'd feel better, too, because I know we started a new routine where I'd be in charge of calling up the suppliers and keeping the shelves full, but it isn't working. If, perhaps, I could have a key to it, or if we could move it so that it's in the same room as me, I think I could keep better tabs on it. But, as it is right now, I'm not there when I'm working in the other room.	Result: feels understood, heard Willing to give opinion (still tentative)
Manager:	So, you say a lot of other people are coming in and just helping themselves. When is that happening? How could we deal with it?	Reflect content; seek information; invite data

		Skills and results
Clerk:	Well, I guess they don't want to sign things out with me. Or, they just want free access. Or, maybe they feel they don't want to ask me. I'm not sure. But another problem we've got is that I can't keep enough backlog. I don't really have the budget to get enough supplies so that we've got at least two or three months supply in advance. Especially the tapes. Many people are using the tapes now, and I haven't got enough money to order enough at one time.	Result: willing to give opinion and give information
Manager:	Okay. It seems to me that there are a couple of problems in this situation. One, maybe we have to make it more difficult for people to get access and give you a little bit more authority there. Is that what you're saying? And the second thing is that we are having some difficulties with the suppliers. I will take care of the first very simply. I'll send out a memo advising people of the new procedures and request that they now go through you to requisition supplies and equipment. And I'll give you a key to the storage rooms. Are there any other ways?	Reflect content, don't react Be tentative Give decision; declare your stand Model flexibility Seek information
Clerk:	You know what would be helpful, too? Some people don't let me know too much in advance — especially when they're going to use more tapes for a program. If I could have a general list from them of their plans in advance, then I would have a better idea, too, of what to order. As it is, it's just by guess, for me. I don't have an idea what people want.	Result: willing to give information State needs
Manager:	So, you'd like to take a survey in order to plan your inventory, is that it? I agree with you that we need to establish our needs in order to offer better service. Now, what can we do to deal with the suppliers?	Demonstrate listening: reflect content Give opinion Seek information; invite data
Clerk:	The suppliers are slow. But I feel that if I could order more from them at one time, maybe I could get better service. So, the survey will help there, too. I will need a bigger budget, though.	Result: willing to give opinion State needs
Manager:	Okay. I'll check on the budget problems for you once I have your estimate of the inventory needs. Is there anything else that you feel you could do in addition to speed up the suppliers?	Give decision: unambiguous, brief Model flexibility Seek information

69

		Skills and results
Clerk:	Well, gee, I'm not sure . . . Maybe...I do phone them, but I always feel that they don't listen to me, you know. I don't feel I have enough clout with them.	Result: willing to share feelings (even tentatively)
Manager:	I see. You seem to be feeling a little nervous about dealing with them.	Reflect feelings; label
Clerk:	I guess that's it. I could never answer all their questions. I mean there's so much new stuff on the market....	Result: feels understood
Manager:	There are usually brochures and catalogues available from each supplier. Have you seen them?	Give information, not advice
Clerk:	No, I didn't realize that. Hey! If I get the catalogues from them, that would probably help me draw up a good survey for our staff. Then I'd be a lot more familiar with all the products too. And when I can give them bigger orders, I think I'll be able to handle the suppliers better.	Result: increasing confidence, making own decisions
Manager:	Sounds like a good idea. I think you're well on the way to solving our problem. Okay. Here's what we'll do. I'll send a memo and get you a key. You draw up the survey when you've got the catalogues.	Give compliment; describe Give your decision; declare your stand
Clerk:	Okay.	
Manager:	When do you think you'd be ready to give me an inventory estimate?	Seek information State expectations
Clerk:	I could have it completed in two weeks.	Result: increased self-esteem
Manager:	Great. Then let's get together again on this issue in two weeks at the same time and see where we go from there.	State expectations
Clerk:	Sounds good. I think this is going to work a lot better. Thanks a lot.	Result: increased self-esteem
Manager:	Thanks.	

and then in any subsequent discussions. Exhaust all possible obstacles that could be blocking good performance, offer assistance where appropriate, develop and confirm action plans.

This does not mean that it is never the employee's fault or that you never focus on the employee's competency. You can always go the competency route later. If you do so too early, however, you may lose out on solving the real problems and create a lot of other problems for yourself.

When the performance problem persists, agreements are not met, and there is no other possible systems explanation for poor performance, then it's time to focus on the person's competency. When you do, you'll find that you can deal with it without the anger and anxiety that usually accompany such a discussion.

By describing the lack of improvement and its impact, now clearly documented, your criticism and disciplinary actions cannot be easily disputed. You may (and probably will) still face manipulative tactics. Keep focused on your stated needs and expectations; ignore the manipulative attacks; don't challenge the irrelevant (see Sample #4.)

Try Worksheet #18 to test your skills in dealing with a poor performer.

3. Tips for dealing with a poor performer

- Focus on the problem, not the person.
- Describe your observations and the impact.
- Seek information.
- Reflect feelings and content.
- State your needs.
- Offer your help.
- Agree on the steps each of you will take.
- Set a follow-up date.

Chapter 5 reading list

Bradford, David L. and Allan R. Cohen. *Managing For Excellence: The Guide to developing High Performance in Contemporary Organizations.* New York: John Wiley & Sons, 1984.

Kriegel, Robert, and Marilyn Harris Kriegel. *The C-Zone: Peak Performance Under Pressure.* New York: Anchor Press, 1984.

HANDLING PERFORMANCE PROBLEMS — LACK OF IMPROVEMENT

Manager to the same clerk, Kelly, at a later time after several discussions		
		Skills used
Manager:	When I went to get some equipment today, it wasn't stocked. I need to be able to count on adequate supplies at all times.	Give criticism State needs; focus
Clerk:	Well, you know, I've been busy, so I let people help themselves. It was a lot of hassle, you know.	
Manager:	As I recall, we had agreed to keep it locked and use the new requisition procedure. I need to be able to count on....	Give information State needs
Clerk:	Well, I lost the key and it takes too much time....	
Manager:	That may be so. Nevertheless, I need to be able to count on....	Ignore challenge
Clerk:	And besides, the suppliers are too slow.	
Manager:	I have kept some notes. All supplies that were ordered were delivered on time. When you don't keep up to date on the orders, they don't deliver. Our staff is caught short and cannot work without the equipment and supplies they need. I need to be able....	Give information Give criticism Describe impact State needs
Clerk:	Well, I don't know....	
Manager:	I require someone in the job who will.... You've shown that you can't or won't. For that reason, I've decided to let you go.	State needs Give decision

WORKSHEET #18
DEALING WITH A POOR PERFORMER

1. Describe a performance problem that one of your subordinates has. Give examples of the impact on you and your department.

_____

_____

_____

_____

_____

_____

2. Imagine that this person is now in front of you. You have decided to discuss the issue for the first time. Write out your opening statement. Use your actual dialogue.

_____

_____

_____

_____

_____

_____

3. Practice two or three versions of different statements you will make to possible responses from the other person. Use the assertive skills for give and take in.

_____

_____

_____

_____

_____

_____

6
SETTING GOALS THAT WORK

"Just keep up the good work."

"I'd like to see things change in the future."

"Do the best you can."

"You've got to make the quota this month."

These statements reflect the way many goal-setting discussions take place between managers and their employees. Unfortunately, too, they often represent the beginning and the end of the discussion.

Goals can be a powerful motivating tool when goal-setting is handled effectively. Setting goals that work means defining goals in ways that ensure employees understand and accept them. Setting goals that work also means supporting goals in ways that ensure employees can work toward successful accomplishment of them. The basic give and take in assertive skills will help you manage the communication process to handle both of these aspects of good goal-setting effectively.

In Sample #5, listen in on part of a discussion between a manager and his administrative assistant, Frank, as they discuss a new project for Frank. Note the assertive skills used. Later comments will illustrate how the manager plays a critical role in whether or not the goal is achieved.

a. DEFINE SMART GOALS

Work on the communication process until the goals you set with your employees meet these criteria: specific, measurable, attainable, relevant, and time-framed.

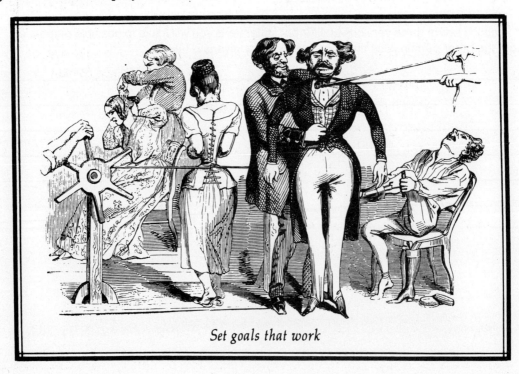

Set goals that work

74

		Skills used
Manager:	As you know, Frank, I've been concerned about the amount of money and time put into training. Yet, I'm not sure we're meeting the needs of our different groups or getting results. I'd like you to take responsibility for looking at the training needs.	Share feelings State expectations
Frank:	That sounds like a hell of an undertaking. Do you mean for the whole staff of 1,100, including the field personnel? That's a big project.	
Manager:	Yes. I know. I can understand your hesitancy. I'm a little overwhelmed by the project myself. This is the first time we're attempting to coordinate all the training offered and carried out on a more inte-grated basis.	Reflect feelings and label Give information
Frank:	So, what you want me to do is see how the programs are working, is that it?	
Manager:	No, at least not at first, not at this stage. I don't want to evaluate the present programs until I know what the needs are. Some evaluative comments may come up, in fact, I'm sure they will, but that's not the main objective of this project.	Give information to correct interpretation State needs; focus
Frank:	Why is it a problem now?	
Manager:	Many of our field staff have had to be retrained by the area managers. Also, there's been a lot of duplication of some of the sessions. I don't think we're making the best use of our resources.	Give information Give opinion
Frank:	I see. So, then, I should aim at analyzing training needs for the company as a whole and try to find some common patterns across the groups and identify some unique needs.	
Manager:	Yes. That's it. How do you feel about taking on the project yourself?	Seek information
Frank:	Well, I've had some experience, but not on this scale — I mean with so many different groups involved. I don't know. One project I did once on the same idea took a month just for one depart-ment. The interviews take time to set up and carry out.	

		Skills used
Manager:	You've been particularly effective in organizing major projects in the past, like the computer needs assessment. You gained a lot of support from others the way you brought in their views. You're mainly concerned about being overwhelmed, is that it?	Give compliment; use examples Reflect content
Frank:	Yes. I guess that's it. How soon do you want it completed?	
Manager:	Our major training starts up each fall about mid-September. We want to avoid duplication this year and get better results.	Give information; not advice
Frank:	So, if I could have the project completed by early May, you could use the results for planning the fall programs.	
Manager:	Yes. I want to be able to do that. Let's see, it's now mid-February. When could you have a draft ready of your plan of attack?	State needs Seek information
Frank:	I could have it ready by next week. I could meet you with it Tuesday afternoon.	
Manager:	Good. Then let's get together at 2:30, Tuesday, to okay the plan for the project. I'd also like to hear from you, at that time, how I could be of help to you.	Seek information
Frank:	Okay. I'll take responsibility for planning and carrying out the training needs analysis by May 15, at the latest. And, I'll schedule for the project next Tuesday and let you know what help I need — doors opened, some facts on future plans, etc.	
Manager:	Great. In the meantime, I'll make the announcement in the manager's memo due out on Friday so others will be aware of the project and ready to support you.	Give decision; declare your stand

1. Specific goals

Both the manager and the employee in the example shared views, facts, feelings, and needs until the goal was clearly understood as a specific, manageable piece of work.

Not being sure what is really supposed to be done is a major source of stress on the job for many employees. It is one of the quickest ways to undermine confidence and lower motivation.

State your needs, reflect content and feelings, and give information until the goal is specific enough to work:

"So you want me to see how ...."

"No, not at this stage, until I know what the needs are ...."

"I see, then, I should aim at ...."

2. Measurable goals

The manager and the employee agreed on what factors or activities would indicate progress toward the goal. Clearly defining the checkpoints contributes to understanding and acceptance, not only because it eliminates ambivalence on the part of the employee about how he or she will be evaluated, but because it allows the employee to monitor his or her own progress.

"Find some common patterns across the groups and identify some unique needs."

3. Attainable goals

Both the manager and the employee used knowledge of the employee's past history and current abilities to help him set a challenging goal. Goals that challenge the employee to stretch himself, but are still attainable, work better than goals that are too easily met or that are out of line with an employee's experiences and abilities.

"You've been particularly effective."

"One project I did took a month."

4. Relevant goals

The manager gave enough information to the employee to indicate how the goal fit in to the organization as a whole. The more meaningful the goals to the employee, the more easily understood and accepted. The employee can make better connections with how his or her part in the process will be used by another part of the organization.

"Many of our field staff have had ...."

"There's been a lot of duplication ...."

"Our major training starts up ...."

5. Time-framed goals

The manager and the employee established and agreed to a definite time frame which would meet both their needs. The manager needs the results in order to plan for next fall's training programs. The employee needs a deadline in order to focus and manage his time, but the deadline must allow adequate time to achieve the goal. Goals that have loose or unstated time-frames tend to lose priority and do not work.

"I could have the project completed by early May."

"Let's get together at 2:30, Tuesday."

Note that both the manager and the employee participated in defining the goal. Usually, when employees can contribute their views, facts, feelings, and needs to the goal-setting process, they are more likely to understand, accept, and work toward the goal.

Using assertive skills to manage the goal-setting dialogue assures that employees' contributions will be taken in. This results in enhanced self-esteem, increased commitment, and increased willingness to accept challenging assignments.

b. SUPPORT GOALS TO ACHIEVE RESULTS

As activity gets underway, use your assertive skills with the employee concerned and with others in your organization to ensure the support necessary for goal achievement. Some of the ways you can contribute to effective goal achievement include the following.

1. Maintain support

Field studies have shown that managers who maintain continued interest in progress toward the goals of their employees achieve better results than those who help define equally clear goals but then withdraw — figuratively, if not physically. It's tempting to think that it's someone else's responsibility now and withdraw or think it'd be quicker to do it yourself and take over.

As your employees meet triumphs and trials along the way, use your assertive skills to demonstrate ongoing supportiveness by listening uncritically, questioning, and supporting them in their dilemmas (see Sample #6).

Nurture and guide the progress toward goals with feedback against checkpoints and recognition for accomplishments. Use your skills to give criticism and compliments effectively (see Sample #7).

2. Open doors

Many goals-in-progress falter because of inadequate supplies, incomplete information, unavailable contacts, needed equipment, etc. Use your assertive skills with others in the organization to facilitate adequate resources, increase awareness of projects, and enlist others' cooperation. It helps to think of yourself as a resource broker for your employees. Remember that one of your most valuable resources is the communication process with them and with others (see Sample #8).

3. Encourage planning skills

Employees will experience more success in achieving goals if they have a logical, step-by-step action plan clearly in mind. As a manager, you can help develop the analytical and decision-making skills necessary for them to define action plans if you make it a stated part of your expectations.

SAMPLE #6
DEMONSTRATE ONGOING SUPPORT

		Skills used
Frank:	I'm really having a tough time setting up interviews with the field supervisors. They just don't want to spend the time.	
Manager:	You sound pretty discouraged. What timing do you give them? (NOT: Why don't you ....?)	Show empathy Seek information
Frank:	I need an hour for each one.	
Manager:	Hmm. Are the questions similar for each one?	Seek information
Frank:	Yeah, they are. Hey! What if I got three or four of them together at a time...and then...I wonder how that would work.	
Manager:	You mean there's some common ground to cover and that would cut down on the one-on-one time, is that it?	Demonstrate listening; reflect content
Frank:	Yes. I see how I could do it!	

		Skills used
Manager:	When you don't let the field supervisors know well enough in advance, they get annoyed because they can't fit it into their schedules. (NOT: You never gave them enough time.)	Give criticism; describe examples and impact
Frank:	You're right. I guess I'll have to get better organized.	

Use your assertive skills to ask the right questions, share your feelings, and give information to encourage the action planning process. Being a manager, you are probably more familiar with the problem or project at hand, have a larger overview, and have more experience. However, resist the temptation to take over responsibility for this part of the goal-setting process. By taking time to take in views and feelings, consider, and facilitate the learning of the planning skills, you develop valuable resources in your employees for the future, and they gain increased commitment to their goals (see Sample #9).

Try Worksheet #19 to test your skills in helping with goal setting.

4. **Tips for setting goals that work**

- Define SMART goals
  - (a) Specific
  - (b) Measurable
  - (c) Attainable
  - (d) Relevant
  - (e) Time-framed
- Provide support
  - (a) Maintain ongoing interest
  - (b) Give feedback
  - (c) Give recognition
  - (d) Open doors
  - (e) Encourage planning skills

ENCOURAGE COMMUNICATION AND COOPERATION

		Skills used
Manager:	(to another department head) Les, I'd like to be able to give Frank the new product estimates for the fall. He would get further with the field personnel on the needs assessment. Will you let him have some of the information, even in draft form if necessary?	State needs Give information
	OR	
Manager:	(in the manager's meeting) I'm very pleased with the way the training needs assessment is shaping up. Frank has incorporated a lot of the initial information you gave him into the survey. He will be contacting you to set up appointments. I'd like your cooperation in getting them finished as soon as possible.	Share feelings Give information State expectations

SAMPLE #9
ENCOURAGE PLANNING SKILLS

		Skills used
Frank:	How should I organize this survey?	
Manager:	What options do you have? (NOT: Well, you should ...)	Seek information
Frank:	Maybe I could modify the design from the needs assessment I worked on for computer needs. I'm just not sure I'm going to cover everything.	
Manager:	How would you know?	Seek information
Frank:	Well, I guess I could check with the heads of each group when I've got it ready.	
Manager:	That sounds like a good idea. Many of them are doing budget plans today and tomorrow.	Give information; not advice
Frank:	Okay. If I draft it up, then see the department heads to check it out first, by that time I'll be in a better	

WORKSHEET #19
GOAL SETTING

Follow the steps below to practice the goal setting process for one of your employees.

1. Think of a project, assignment, standard, or quota you would like to define with one of your employees. How is this project defined in your own mind? What do you actually want achieved as an end result?

_____

_____

2. Pretend the employee is with you now. Write out your opening statement. Use your actual words in order to practice the language of assertive skills.

_____

_____

3. Demonstrate with actual dialogue how you will respond to two or three concerns the employee might have.

_____

_____

_____

4. Write out a well-defined goal statement that could represent the goal you and your employee finally agree upon.

_____

_____

5. Write out at least one statement to demonstrate how you would open doors.

_____

_____

_____

6. Write out at least one statement to demonstrate how you would encourage planning skills in your employee.

_____

_____

_____

Chapter 6 reading list

Locke, Edwin A., and Gary P. Latham. *Goal Setting: A Motivational Technique That Works.* Englewood Cliffs, N.J.: Prentice Hall, 1984.

McCall, Morgan W., Jr., Michael M. Lombardo, and Ann M. Morrison. *The Lessons of Experience: How Successful Executives Develop on the Job.* Lexington, Mass.: Lexington Books, 1988.

7

THE MANAGER AS CAREER COACH

"But I chat with my employees when we do our yearly review. Isn't that enough?"

"I've always said they can come and see me any time. What more can I do?"

"Shouldn't they take the opportunities we give them?"

These statements, unfortunately, reflect the attitudes many managers have held toward developing the careers of their staff. In the 1990s, however, the manager has a new role to play: career coach.

Employees want to take charge of their work lives to create a more satisfying challenge to their interests and their abilities. They want to achieve a better balance between their work lives and their private and family lives. However, in order to carry out these values based on responsible choices, employees need new and different kinds of resources. They need opportunities and information presented in a way that has not been a tradition with organizations in the past. They need to remain in charge of their choices.

a. OPPORTUNITY LOST

Consider the following short case description of what happened between one manager, Tom, and one of his most valued employees, Steve.*

Tom Ellery was vice-president of sales and Steve Watson was a regional sales manager in charge of four district managers. Steve reported to one of the three area managers who, in turn, reported to Tom. Tom had followed Steve's career with interest and considered him one of the best sales managers in the company. It was not surprising, then, that Steve's name came immediately to mind when Tom received a memo from the marketing VP asking for recommendations for someone to take over the marketing services department.

Marketing services employed about 400 people and provided promotional support and special services to the sales division. In salary grade, the position was one level higher than regional sales manager, so it would offer Steve a promotion. Tom thought Steve was the ideal candidate for the job for several reasons. First, people in both the marketing and sales divisions felt marketing services had become unresponsive to the sales division's needs. The department was now more of a bottleneck than a service, and Steve's extensive experience as a sales manager would give him a clear idea of what kind of support the department ought to be giving.

Second, the department had begun to suffer from an "image problem," which Steve's transfer could do much to correct. Marketing services had developed a reputation for being a place where people were assigned when they ceased being effective in product management or in field sales. Putting an acknowledged "comer" like Steve in charge of the department would go far toward dispelling that image.

---

*From John J. Gabarro, "Understanding Communication in One to One Relationships," 9-476-075. Copyright © 1975 by the President and Fellows of Harvard College. Reprinted by permission of the Harvard Business School.

The position would also provide Steve with an opportunity for wider corporate exposure and the ability to influence total company marketing and sales efforts.

After consulting with the marketing VP, Tom sent Steve a copy of the original memo, with the added note, "Are you interested? I think you're the best person for the job. Come by and let's talk about it." Tom was pleased that his own division was finally strong enough to allow him the flexibility to offer one of his best people to another division. It had taken three years of systematically identifying weak spots and moving strong new people like Steve into them to provide this luxury, and he planned to make the most of it.

Pause for a moment before you read on and consider what assumptions Steve might make on receiving the memo and what his feelings might be. Note them briefly on a separate sheet of paper.

A few days later, Steve came by to discuss the memo. Tom was surprised to find Steve uninterested in the transfer, and slightly curt and ill at ease as well. Steve began by saying he didn't think he had the background to do the job and that he still had a lot to do in the region before he felt he could move on to another position.

Sensing that Steve might be a little anxious about moving into the marketing division, Tom went into more detail on the reasons why he thought Steve could handle the job and do it well. Steve remained unconvinced, however, and as a last resort Tom suggested that Steve talk with the marketing VP before making a final decision. Tom couldn't help feeling annoyed at the end of the conversation, and found himself questioning his original judgments about Steve's flexibility and adaptability.

Pause for a moment more and consider what inferences and assumptions Tom is making about Steve's response, and why they lead to feelings of annoyance.

Tom's disappointment continued. Steve's talk with the marketing VP failed to change his mind, and Tom began to feel his relationship with Steve becoming strained. Soon Tom noticed Steve was avoiding him and seemed especially silent in his presence. About a month later, Tom received a call from Steve's area manager saying that Steve had resigned to take a position with a competitor.

Consider what perceptions and assumptions could lie behind Steve's action. How do you sense Steve feels in taking such an action?

Tom later learned from a mutual friend that Steve had left because he had concluded that his career with the company was finished when Tom offered him the marketing services job.

Did you deduce this from what went before? How do you think Tom felt when he heard the news?

This case, adapted from a real experience, illustrates many mistakes common to managers handling career discussions and decisions with their employees.

1. The mistakes

Tom doesn't *give* and *take in* effectively.

(a) He doesn't give needed information about the company's recognition of marketing services as "outer Siberia" and their decision to turn it around.

(b) He doesn't share his feelings, his pleasure, and pride in having a strong division from which he can send someone in this difficult challenge.

(c) He doesn't give examples of "why you're the best person for the job" at the appropriate time.

(d) He doesn't take in and acknowledge Steve's discomfort; he discounts

Steve's feelings by going into more detail.

(e) He doesn't take in and reflect back Steve's objections; he reacts to them with "go talk to the marketing VP."

Tom's biggest mistake is not being responsive. Even if he gave Steve the added information about his reasons for wanting Steve in the job, he would do so in a way and at a time when Steve could not hear him. The issue of Steve's distress was never addressed. This is the issue blocking the communication process. Tom had his decision made, so he reacted to the block defensively at first by justifying and explaining and then aggressively with annoyance and anger. "Why is he resisting me? Doesn't he realize what a good move this is?"

For Steve, the situation moves from bad to worse. Because his concerns are discounted or rationalized by Tom, he's more convinced he is right. He begins to doubt his own abilities and his perception of his worth, and he questions his interpretation of the company's perception of his worth. He retreats, becomes defensive to protect himself, and quits before they can get him.

2. The results

(a) Steve misses out on what could have been a valuable and challenging career opportunity.

(b) Tom questions his effectiveness as a manager; was he wrong in his judgments or in his handling of the situation?

(c) The company loses resources: time, energy, and talent while both continue on the job in their state of anxiety, guilt, and anger, and, ultimately, a valuable employee.

Steve lacks assertive skills as well. However, as a manager, you are responsible for carrying out your part of the dialogue effectively. You can use your assertive skills to manage this process of discussion, dilemma, and decision while not taking over responsibility for the decision or opting out because it's not your job.

b. OPPORTUNITIES FOUND: USING ASSERTIVE SKILLS TO COACH CAREERS

1. Give information

Tom: Steve, one of the organizational decision's we've recently made is to make marketing services more responsive to the sales division's needs.

Steve: Well, yes, I guess that has been one of our problems in sales.

Tom: I agree. I also think it's not going to be an easy task.

Employees need information concerning the organization's goals and future trends in order to make responsible choices. When you assume you know what's best for employees (as Tom did with Steve), you may easily overlook the fact that they need some of the background information that led you to take over the decision for them.

An effective career coach gives information in ways that provide employees with the relevant facts they need concerning the organization and the jobs. They talk about job listings, job descriptions, staff roles, career paths and logical cross-over points, reporting relationships, and so on without showing a bias or giving advice.

An effective career coach also gives information concerning the political realities of how things get done in the organization; which types of programs or projects got supported by whom; how long decisions take; how others have gained visibility and support; where to look for special alliances or needed information, etc.

Tom: In the past, it has looked like a move to marketing services meant being sent out to pasture. We want to turn that image around.

Steve: So, then, that's not what's happening to me. You mean I can start a new trend if I can pull it off!

Effective employees are those committed to their choices. They can't be committed if they have been intimidated, coerced, persuaded, or pushed into choices they do not own. By giving the relevant information or providing access to it, you are developing employees' skills to assess, analyze, and draw conclusions, and match it against their own goals and abilities.

2. Support self-appraisal

Steve: I'm not sure I'm interested in the job.

Tom: You mean you don't think you have the experience to do it, is that it?

(NOT: Of course you are. Just go talk to the VP of marketing.)

Steve: Well, it's not that so much. I guess I could do it. But, well, I just don't think it's the job for me.

Tom: You seem pretty reluctant to talk about marketing services.

Steve: Yeah, I don't like it much.

Tom: What is it about marketing services that's turned you off?

(NOT: Why don't you? or Sure, you'll like it. You just haven't tried it, that's all.)

Here Tom could begin to give more information concerning the organization's goals for marketing services or he could continue to explore, seek information, and reflect. Steve's concerns about his future need to be acknowledged before he can listen to and consider the information undefensively.

Employees can make more effective career decisions when they have a thorough understanding of themselves. As a career coach, you can do a lot to provide ways for employees to assess their strengths and weaknesses, the skills they have, and those they want to develop. Your involvement may be minimal or more active. You can demonstrate support for self-appraisal by making career planning workshops available (in house or from outside sources) to your staff and encouraging them to attend.

You can also demonstrate support by providing independent workbooks that take a minimum of orientation time on your part. If you choose these low involvement routes, the way you give your views and state your expectations will convey the measure of your support:

> I think this workbook will make it easier for you to plan your future. It's an excellent first step. Before we talk about your career, I'd like you to finish the first part on self-assessment.

Support self-appraisal

(NOT: There's some workbooks available on career planning for those who want to take a look.)

On the other hand, you may become more actively involved in supporting the self-assessment process. Some departments have developed team workshops with the manager assisting in exercises and discussions on a regular basis, for example, two hours a week for four or five weeks.

Whatever the level of involvement, an effective career coach will also act as a sounding board once the self-assessment process is well under way. Use your assertive skills in giving feedback to let employees test their perceptions of their skills and strengths against your knowledge of their abilities. Use your assertive skills in listening to acknowledge and take in their hopes and concerns. You can act as a reality test before they set career goals for themselves.

Clerk: I'd like to get into Personnel. I think I'd be really good with people.

Manager: When you get a client here who's dissatisfied, I notice that you often ask Mary to take over.

Clerk: Oh, I know, but that's different. I could do it in Personnel. I mean, then it's our employees you're talking to.

Manager: What is it about some of the clients that makes them hard for you to handle?

Clerk: Well, when they're really mad about something or when somebody's really frustrated and upset, I guess I think I won't be able to satisfy them.

Manager: Do you think employees who are unhappy or upset might act differently?

Clerk: Hmmm…well, maybe not. I see what you mean.

Manager: I think you need to test out your ability to handle people who are difficult. When you

have followed through yourself with a few clients who are unhappy and have problems, I'd like to talk to you again.

In this role, you will need some new information yourself. To be an effective career coach, you need to actively and assertively seek information about such things as the concerns that arise at different career stages, factors that affect career transitions, or dual career dilemmas. Then, you can be responsive; you can take in concerns or views and values different from your own with genuine support and understanding.

3. Support multiple options

Tom: It's a good opportunity for a promotion for you, Steve.

Steve: Yes, I agree it's good. I feel I'm in a dilemma, though. I know what the job would involve in terms of hours and travel and I'm not sure I want that right now.

Tom: I see, so it's not the challenge that's making you hesitate, it's the timing, is that it?

(NOT: You're not scared of a little hard work are you? This could really set you up.)

Steve: Yes. I like the challenge of it. I like the work. I know I could do it. What bothers me is the time away from home. We've got two small kids, you know. I'd be happier to find ways to open up my present job a little. I think there's a lot I could do there still.

Tom: I'd like to hear about that.

There are other ways to be successful than the traditional operation of moving up. Many employees, and managers too, are part of the values shift away from work as the center of life toward wanting a better balance with one's whole life.

An effective career coach will credit these other options as much as upward mobility. Your employees need information about lateral moves, exploratory opportunities to test out other areas, downward moves, and job enrichment possibilities in order to make satisfying career decisions. You can support their decision dilemmas by listening uncritically during career planning discussions even when it's not what you would do yourself or what you would plan for them. Valuing differences in lifestyles and aspirations is a key part of being an effective career coach.

In addition to recognizing and making more career options available, an effective career coach will encourage employees to make plans to pursue more than one option at a time. The pace of change in the 1990s demands flexibility. In your discussions, you can set expectations that an employee who, for example, defines career goals in a lateral area also pursues new challenges in his or her present job with an enrichment plan. This develops skills that may or may not be used in the next career choice area but, in so doing, develops an increased sense of competency for the employee. Employees who have multiple options feel less threatened by possible obsolescence. They generally experience a greater sense of control over their lives and less stress, and, as a result, are more willing to accept challenging assignments.

Support your belief in multiple career options by stating your view in other parts of the organization, thus possibly opening doors for your staff to test out opportunities.

Support multiple career options with your staff by rewarding such planning: give verbal recognition and provide needed training and other resources when appropriate.

You can enjoy the career planning discussion with your employees. You are not responsible for their decisions. You are a catalyst. You are responsible for using the communication process effectively so that your employees can make satisfying, responsible decisions. You can do this by using your assertive skills to ensure that —

(a) all relevant information needs are met,

(b) employees have a reality-tested self-assessment profile, and

(c) multiple career options are considered and pursued.

Try Worksheet #20 to test your skills as a career coach.

4. Tips for being an effective career coach

- Open doors
- Support self-appraisal
- Be a good sounding board; value differences
- Support multiple career options

WORKSHEET # 20
CAREER PLANNING

1. Think of an employee you have had a career planning discussion with in the past. Describe the situation. How did you handle it? How did you feel? How did the employee handle it? What were the results?

_____

_____

_____

_____

2. Replay the discussion now. Write your opening statement to the employee. Use the actual words.

_____

_____

3. Practice two or three different responses to statements the employee might make.

_____

_____

_____

_____

4. How do you respond to these common statements from employees: "Do you think I should get an accounting degree?"

_____

_____

5. "I thought I'd be able to learn Mary's job. I want more to do."

_____

_____

6. "Unless my wife can find a good job there, too, I'm not sure I want the transfer."

_____

_____

_____

Chapter 7 reading list

Athos, Anthony and John Gabarro. *Interpersonal Behavior: Communication and Understanding in Relationships.* Prentice-Hall, Inc., Englewood Cliffs, N.J., 1978. This is an excellent reference book. The case used in this chapter is taken from it by permission of Prentice-Hall, Inc.

Derr, C. Brooklyn. *Managing the New Careerists.* San Francisco: Jossey-Boss, Inc., 1986.

Jones, Pamela R., Beverly Kaye and Hugh R. Taylor, "You Want Me To Do What?" *Training and Development Journal,* July, 1981, pp. 56-62. This article provides a rationale for the new role of the manager as career coach. It describes the competencies needed and gives examples of different ways the role has been carried out and supported within organizations.

Kaye, Beverly L., "How You Can Help Employees Formulate Their Career Goals." *Personnel Journal,* May, 1980, pp. 368-373. This article provides valuable step-by-step illustrations of how managers can help employees define and test their career goals without making the decisions for them. The examples provide illustrations of a number of different career goal options.

8
PUT YOUR SKILLS TO WORK AT WORK

a. TAKE MORE THAN YOUR SKILLS WITH YOU INTO THE 1990s

Throughout the 1980s, most managers attended a variety of training sessions and picked up numerous "how to" professional development books. Now managers walk around the workplace with quite a sophisticated set of skills in their interpersonal "toolbox"— negotiation skills, goal setting skills, listening skills, and presentation skills. However, even with all their well-polished skills at the ready, managers can still be ineffective, especially if they use these skills for the wrong reasons.

Even though you practiced the basic give and take in assertive skills in chapters 3 and 4, you, too, could still be an ineffective manager if you do not answer three critical questions before you put your skills to work in the workplace:

(a) What is your intent?

(b) Who's in charge (of you)? and

(c) What are you creating?

Let's look at each of these questions separately. This will help you get more out of the case situations later in this chapter.

1. What is your intent?

For what purpose do you want to use your assertive skills with others? To compete more effectively? To control others or the situation more tightly? To protect yourself from failure? To protect your status and authority from being challenged? To look good — even at someone else's expense? Or, to develop, to help yourself and others learn, to enhance capacity — for yourself and for others — to do and be the best possible. Only an intent to develop will be experienced by others as one that demonstrates integrity and will encourage them to make a choice to work with you rather than protect themselves or resist you and your projects.

The actual words you use in a dialogue with others may sound the same no matter your intent. What will affect your ongoing effectiveness with others is how "clean," i.e., nonmanipulative, your intent is. Consider people you have watched at work who demonstrated sophisticated interpersonal skills but you felt their underlying intent was out of line. There was another purpose behind their words. When they made a mistake, how willing were you to forgive and help them recover? Now, consider people at work whose intent was clean (honest, focused on development and learning). When these people made a mistake, how willing were you to forgive and help them recover?

What is your intent when you deal with others, regardless of the degree of skill you possess in your interactions with them? When your intent has integrity, you don't need perfectly polished skills. Others will recognize your intent to develop and be more likely to help you and to learn from the situation.

Given the need for trust, commitment, and improved results in our organizations, you will need to examine the issue of intent carefully for yourself if you really want these assertive skills to work for you in the long run.

An intent to develop, to learn, and to enhance capacity is part of a general shift in the 1990s toward a new description of the organization as a "learning organization," where the manager is seen as a "coach" or a "manager-as-developer." Your organization can't truly be a "learning organization" if its systems and structures continue to set up expectation and reward for destructive competitiveness among its groups or departments. You can't be an effective manager if both your company's structures and your intent as a manager are towards control, judgment, and blame, regardless of your skill level.

In the case scenarios presented in Worksheets #21 to #28 in this chapter, the issue of intent will be in question as you decide what your focus is before you begin your discussion with another person. For example, if your focus in a discussion is to make sure somebody else admit he or she is wrong, then the intent behind it is more closely linked to "being right" or "having control" than to "development, learning, and enhancing capacity." While you may use one of the assertive skills with the right words, the discussion may be more guarded or reactive and your long-term effectiveness will likely be undermined.

Also, if you think you *need to protect yourself* with an intent such as "being right," then move on to the second of the three critical questions.

2. Who's in charge?

This is a question about who's in charge of you — not your office or your department. Think about people in your work life who make you angry, make you nervous, anxious, frustrated, or wary. When you speak with that person, who is in charge of defining how you are going to respond? If you find yourself yelling back because "Bob makes me so angry" or getting stuck on arguing minute details because "I need Jan to think I know what I'm talking about," who is in charge of you? Not you. In the first instance it's Bob. He is defining how you will behave because you are reacting to his style instead of staying in charge and deciding for yourself how you want to act. In the second instance it's Jan. She is defining how you act because, again, you are reacting to your need to prove something to her rather than deciding for yourself how you want to act.

Understanding this question will help you understand how a statement can be assertive in one situation, and nonassertive (either passive or aggressive) in another. In the same way, in some situations, remaining silent can be assertive and in others nonassertive. At any given moment if you find yourself in a reactive pattern, either making a statement or remaining silent because of somebody else, perhaps because of intimidation or guilt, then you are not in charge of you and you are not demonstrating an assertive stance. At any given moment if you make a statement or remain silent out of free choice — conscious awareness to do just what you did with a clean intent — then you are in charge of you and you are demonstrating an assertive stance.

This is a key question for the manager in the nineties. Managers need to have all of their energy available to meet the current demand for creativity, flexibility, and care. Managers need presence in order to be effective. When you spend too much time in reactive patterns — the "not-in-charge-of-you" mode — you are likely to end your day feeling fragmented and exhausted. After all, you have spent the day being defined by dozens of different people as you reacted to their various expectations and personality quirks. When you can stay in charge of you for more moments in your day, regardless of what other people do, you will experience more clarity, stay more focused, have more energy, and enjoy an increased capacity to be "spontaneously appropriate."

In the case situations you can work on in this chapter, you will be identifying what a problem situation needs in order to break out of a stuck cycle and get to first base. You will also identify what's at stake for you.

Knowing what's at stake for you means knowing what you are afraid of: for example, losing control, having your status challenged, being too visible, failing, etc. These worksheet questions are related to the more fundamental question of "Who's in charge of you?"

When you can identify how a problem stays stuck (e.g., "I always get defensive when she criticizes my work and then I go silent,") and when you can identify what's at stake for you (e.g., "needing to be right/perfect"), you are in a better position to make a new choice that puts you back in charge of you. Just being aware of the pattern and your own issues and needs will help you have the courage to risk a new behavior and use one of the assertive skills that will get you to first base.

Remember, "If you always do what you've always done, you'll always get what you've always got." Effective managers in the nineties need to do some new things in order to create some different results. And that brings us to the third critical question.

3.   What are you creating?

With the pressure and the pace in today's workplace, many managers lose their awareness of what they are creating because of the

Spending too much time in reactive patterns will make you feel fragmented and exhausted.

way they handle situations and people. Difficult people or poor performers are discredited with such comments as "That's just the way he is" or "Everybody knows she's like that;" the level of innovation evident in a work project is assumed to be all that's available; procedures and policies are followed out of "habit" because "That's what we always do;" high levels of personal stress are accepted as "part of being successful." These results are often accepted as "given."

In every communication, you are responsible for how you handle your part of it. You are responsible for whether you walk away with your self-respect intact and without leftover anger or anxiety draining your energy. You may or may not solve the problem, or make changes happen. You can't assume 100 percent responsibility for that. You can't make your silent staff speak up; you can't make your reluctant employee take part in setting goals; you can't make your coworker change a negative attitude; you can't make your superior change his or her intimidating tactics; you can't make your client stop shouting. But you are responsible for *your* choices. You can decide how to handle the communication process from your end to get the results you want.

Your first priority is to be able to say to yourself, "I handled that well." In the face of manipulation, maintaining your own self-respect may be all you end up with. However, this is more than you'll gain by playing along with manipulation and perpetuating the pattern. In the short run, this may "feel good" to you. However, for the long term not much is learned — for you, the others, or for the work project and the organization as a whole. The results are not effective.

The results of an interaction, particularly the results for the individuals involved and the results for the relationship, are rarely addressed consciously. If they are, they may be addressed after the fact with such comments as "I felt stressed by the way I argued my point until they agreed," "Well, I sure don't trust him very much judging by the way he ran that meeting..." Many managers are managing on "cruise control" or patterns formed from habit and as a result, the "results" just happen. These kinds of results are not necessarily the most effective way to move yourself, others, and your organization along the path of increased learning. No one is taking conscious control in order to create healthier results on a moment-to-moment basis.

A manager who has a strong assertive stance will be much more aware of what he or she wants to create in terms of results for him or herself, for the relationship, and for the work project itself. In addition, this manager is much more aware that the desired results (e.g., "improved level of self-esteem," "more trust in the relationship," "clearer information on a task") are within his or her control and will take conscious charge of creating these results using effective assertive skills.

In the case scenarios in this chapter, you will be asked to identify what you think the results will be based on how you have chosen to deal with a certain problem. This is good discipline to increase your proactive thinking about being in charge of what you are creating.

So you see, as a manager you are taking more than your skills into the nineties in order to be effective. You are also taking a clear intent to use these skills to learn and to develop yourself and others; you are taking a decision to stay in charge of yourself regardless of what others do or in what external situations you find yourself. You are taking an awareness that you are in charge of the results you are creating for yourself, for others, and for the work project itself. With this in mind, let's put the skills to work.

b. DRESS REHEARSAL #1

Remember the manager in chapter 1 who complained of always getting hooked into the same old pattern by the old-timer cynic whenever he tried to introduce a change of procedure to his staff:

> Every time I introduce a new policy or a change of procedure to my staff, one guy, who's been with us about 31 years and resents working for me, always starts in with the same old gripes and criticism about how it's never going to work. I get hooked in justifying and explaining and finally just cut him off by laying down the law.

We'll use this case scenario to work through the same kinds of questions you will answer later on in the other case scenarios. The purpose of this "dress rehearsal" is to help you understand what the questions in Worksheets #21 to #28 mean and to help you realize that there is not just one right answer to a work situation such as this. There can be several very appropriate ways to deal with it. Nevertheless, in order to be appropriate, the way you choose to deal with the situation must take into account the three critical questions discussed at the beginning of this chapter.

For the "old-timer cynic" case scenario above, follow how the five questions used in Worksheets #21 to #28 have been answered.

1. **Focus: What is your focus? Is this a pattern or single event?**

What issue do you want to address? Be careful that you think through which issue, if addressed, would best help you and the other person to learn, to develop, and help the project or task be improved. Having a clearly defined focus helps you stay on track in the discussion, even if the discussion gets heated or the other person becomes manipulative.

In the case of the old-timer cynic (OTC), you could choose from any of the following issues as a central focus. What you choose to focus on will set the theme, or establish a certain pathway, for your discussion.

(a) Making sure he complies with your orders and expectations

If you choose this focus, you may get compliance, but you are not likely to get commitment. Your intent may be seen as "needing to control" or "needing to protect your authority."

Note that your focus could be on getting compliance on this single event or getting compliance in general — that is, dealing with the pattern. In each case scenario you will need to decide whether you want to deal with a pattern or a single event.

(b) Defining and discussing his unsatisfactory behavior

If you choose this focus, you may create more resistance which the OTC could play out in a number of ways: stony silence, withholding information, a direct attack on you, an indirect attack on you through other people, etc. Your intent may be seen as competition: looking for something he's not doing well enough so you can look better.

Note, again, that you could choose to deal with a "single event" incident of unsatisfactory behavior or with the "pattern" of unsatisfactory behavior. The choice you make will create a very different type of discussion.

(c) Helping him use his past experience in a positive way

If you choose this focus, you and he may learn something useful. If you are successful, you may gain valuable information and he will learn how to contribute in a way that will allow him to experience being successful. Even if you aren't successful, your intent is likely to be seen as developmental, non-manipulative, and supportive. Here, again, you could deal with this from a "single event" focus or as a "pattern." In general, people tend to learn more when they can see their own patterns and change them.

2. What's at stake for you in this situation?

This question forces you to become more aware of your own issues and how these issues can keep you in a stuck, reactive pattern with another person. You can't change anything you don't see. So, the first step is to name it. When you can see it, you can usually recognize that someone, or something else, is in charge of you.

For the manager in the case scenario above, some examples might include —

(a) fear of looking incompetent in the eyes of the OTC,

(b) fear of losing control in front of others, and

(c) fear of losing status with peers or with others.

If any one of the above is true for you as the manager, who's in charge of you? Who is defining how you will act and how you will be? Not you — it's the OTC, the others in the group, your peers, etc. This is not an effective way to behave throughout the day. It's also too exhausting. If any one of the above is true for you as the manager, by being more aware of it you can choose to act in a way that minimizes the potential for the "fear" to take over. Seeing it doesn't automatically get rid of it, but seeing it will help you manage your own limitations instead of being controlled by them.

Read the script below which illustrates what a manager might say who has chosen focus (a) above: making sure he complies with orders and expectations.

Manager: (to staff) I'd just like to let you all know this morning that there have been some changes regarding the hiring of outside services. We can't do it on our own any more. If you want outside services, you'll have to put in a requisition with Central Services.

OTC: Oh God, not this trip again. It'll never work.

Manager:	Sure it will. Look, all you have to do is fill in one of these forms, see, turn it in, and it's just about the same thing. *(Defensive, justifying, discounting other's views)*
OTC:	Yeah, all you have to do is wait two years to get any action. I'm not going to fill in all that crap!
Manager:	Come off it! It can't be all that bad. You're exaggerating.
OTC:	Well, if I'm exaggerating, you're naive. You weren't around last time we tried this. *(Aggressive, criticizing, attacking)*
Manager:	Well, I'm here this time and we're going to do it this way. All of us. And that means you, too. That's just the way it is. *(Defensive, intimidating, demanding)*
OTC:	Well, we'll see....

3. What does the situation need in order to get to first base? Do you need to give something more effectively? Do you need to take in something more effectively in order to break the cycle?

In most unproductive, stuck interactions, you can break the cycle by first realizing whether you will need to initiate your discussion with the give skills or with the take in skills. Some managers get stuck and stay stuck because they are consistently *giving out* (opinions or information, for example) when, in fact, they could get to first base more easily if they began by *taking in* (others' feelings or criticism, for example). There is no absolute rule that certain kinds of situations always need you to use one of the give skills first or one of the take in skills first. There are some guidelines that will become clearer as you practice on the case scenarios in this chapter.

In the OTC case scenario above, as manager you would probably get unstuck more effectively if you chose to use one of the take in skills when you first speak directly to the OTC. Often a person who seems to be as resistant as the OTC is dealing with a lot of pent-up emotion. One of the best ways to deal with the emotion and the resistance is to legitimize it, to acknowledge it. The take in assertive skills help you do this effectively. One take in you could use effectively here is *reflect feelings*.

4. Prepare a practice script. Pretend the person is in front of you. What is your opening statement?

This instruction forces you to be clear about your intentions and your focus. In the second dialogue example below, note the first time the manager speaks directly to the OTC: "Ed, you don't seem very pleased..."

This is an example of an opening statement dealing with a focus on helping the OTC make more positive use of his past experience but treating it as a single event, not a pattern.

As the manager, if you chose to deal with this issue as a pattern, you could speak to "Ed the OTC" at another time and in another location but open this discussion with a different statement.

> Ed, one of the things I'm aware of over time with you is that you seem reluctant to give us (or me) the benefit of your experience here, even though you must have some good ideas about our operation. *(Reflect feelings, interpret, label.)*

Imagine two different responses from the other person. Write the dialogue you could use to deal with these responses in a way that keeps the communication process going and builds respect.

In the second dialogue example below, note the ways the manager responds to the OTC. The manager frequently uses a lot of the take in skills. He or she —

(a) seeks information,

(b) takes in criticism, and

(c) reflects content.

When you are faced with resistance, you can usually be more effective by using skills that acknowledge and legitimize it without evaluation.

Read the script below noting how different the results could be based on different choices by the manager.

Manager: (to staff) I have announcements concerning changes in the hiring of outside services. Central Services office will now coordinate all requests. When you need outside services, file a requisition with them on this form. *(Give information.)*

OTC: Oh, God. Not this trip again. It'll never work.

Manager: Ed, you don't seem very pleased with this change in procedure. *(Respond to feelings: acknowledge, reflect, and label.)*

OTC: Well, I'm not. It never worked before and it'll never work now.

Manager: What happened before? I'd like to know. *(Seek information.)*

OTC: Who cares? It's a stupid move.

Manager: That may be so. *(Take in criticism; ignore the challenge.)* We will file requisition forms to Central Services from now on. *(State expectations; keep focused.)* However, I'm also concerned about the potential problems. *(Share feelings.)* What happened last time? *(Seek information.)*

OTC: It takes too long.

Manager: You mean by the time you get approval from Central Services, it's too late for you to make the best use of the outside services, is that it? *(Reflect content.)*

OTC: No, what I mean is it takes half an hour to fill out those dumb forms.

Manager: The forms have been revised. *(Give information.)*

OTC: Oh yeah? Let me see. Yeah, they have. This looks better. It should be okay. Okay, then, I'll go along with you.

Manager: Thanks, I appreciate your input. *(Share feelings.)*

5. **Assess the script you have written, what might be the results — for you? for the relationship? for the work itself?**

When you work on the case scenario worksheets in this chapter, you will only define the results for your effective script. For illustration purposes, let's look at the different results that may be created by each of the dialogues used in this example.

In the first dialogue between the manger and the OTC, the result could be:

- Both people experience a loss of respect — both self-respect and respect for each other

- The communication process is stalemated

- No new information is received

- There is no solution to the problem with the relationship.

Both the manager and the OTC feel frustrated and angry: the manager because he had to pull rank; the OTC because his views and feelings have been discounted.

The manager knows he didn't handle the situation very well. He will now have to invest time to oversee the requisition procedure to make sure it is carried out properly because the OTC doesn't support it and hasn't agreed to it. More than that, he knows the unresolved tension between himself and the OTC will surface to influence their next discussion thus perpetuating the same old unproductive pattern.

There are two ways to understand the OTC. He has a long history with the firm and could share valuable information and feelings concerning the change. How the pattern got started is less important now than the fact that the communication process does not allow for or acknowledge his input. Thus, the resources available for the manager are not as good as they could be. The OTC has an aggressive style himself, but he may be turned around with an effective use of assertive skills by the manager.

On the other hand, the OTC may be deliberately baiting the manager with his manipulative comments and criticism. He may not want to cooperate. When he successfully triggers the same old angry, authoritative outburst from the manager, he feels he's won.

Remember, however, that aggressive behavior stems from anxiety, frustration, and dissatisfaction. In this case, you may or may not be able to deal with whatever is generating the aggressive behavior, but you can handle your side of the dialogue more responsibly. Whichever way you want to understand the behavior, you, at least, can walk away from the situation with your self-respect intact and no leftover smoldering anger.

The results of the second dialogue are:

- Both people have maintained self-respect and respect for the other

- New information is shared

- The problem is solved

- The working relationship is strengthened for the future

There are many responses the manager could have used. This is not the only script possible. What's important is to demonstrate respect for the other's views while not selling out your own. In this case, the other person chose to respond cooperatively to your side of the dialogue.

c. DRESS REHEARSAL #2

What if the person you are having a discussion with refuses to cooperate? Realistically, you can't expect others to change their habit patterns and style just because you are trying a new style. Some will respond and make a new choice for themselves quite readily; others will take longer or choose not to change at all. Either way, you be able to hold to your intent and the focus of your discussion and stay in charge of yourself.

Recall the manager in chapter 1 who complained that every time she tried to work out a decision with her staff, no one spoke up — until later. We can use this work situation to demonstrate how you can stay focused and in charge of yourself in the face of noncooperation on the part of others. It is also another opportunity for you to practice working through the five worksheet questions for the case scenarios that follow.

Manager: So we have to make a decision in our office about something. I call my staff in, ask for their ideas, no one speaks up. Same thing every time. I finally make the decision. They say nothing. Then, when it's too late, when we've set the wheels in motion, I start to get all kinds of flak about it's such a bad idea. Why don't they speak up when I ask them?

This is a common problem and one you're sure to confront in one form or another:

- A reluctant employee, who won't help set goals or expectations, then blames you because your goals are unrealistic for them to achieve.

- A coworker who meets every suggestion or request with an automatic negative before considering the situation or hearing you out fully.

- A supervisor who asks for your input, then carries on controlling the discussion without listening to you.

- An employee who tries to shout you down when you are trying to work through a problem together.

98

The key to handling these types of situations well is to check your focus. The topic of your discussion (the decision or problem you were working on) can no longer be the primary focus of your discussion when you are faced with manipulative tactics that block the communication process. Stop the clock on the topic or content. Address the issue that is getting in the way of getting to first base in your interaction with the other person. You won't be able to resolve the topic or content issue anyway until you do address the process issue.

For example, consider the manager faced with the silent staff.

1. **Focus: What is your focus? Is this a pattern or single event?**

    I want staff to understand and accept my expectation that they work with me by contributing more openly to decision making discussion.

Treat it as a pattern! The intent behind this focus is developmental — to enhance everybody's capacity as you all learn how to work more effectively with each other and learn how to take ownership for what happens in the department.

The employee who tries to shout you down

Notice that, as manager, you are defining this as an expectation you have. This expectation will establish a new pattern for everybody. You are not focusing on a "single event" incident in which staff did not participate well. You are also not focusing on the negative past history pattern that has already happened. Instead you are defining the focus in terms of what you want to create for the future. You will still refer to past history in your discussion, but having a clear focus on what you want to create with them minimizes the danger of getting stuck in blame, judgment, control, and power games.

2. **What's at stake?**

What has kept you stuck in this unproductive cycle? Again, when you understand this issue about yourself more clearly, the concern will have less power over you and be less likely to trip you into a reactive pattern in your discussion with the others. For the manager in the case scenario above, some of the issues might include the following:

(a) Fear of losing control of the situation

(b) Fear of being rejected by staff if a difficult issue is raised

(c) Perfectionism — their ideas might not be suitable and I don't know how to turn them down without creating defensiveness

If any one of these issues is true for you as the manager in this situation, who's in charge of you? Not you — the staff are in charge of defining how you will act and how you will be. This is a very good opportunity for others who want to manipulate you. It is also not an effective way to develop your own capacity or to help others develop themselves.

3. **What does the situation need in order to get to first base? Do you need to give something more effectively? Do you need to take in something more effectively?**

In order to get to first base with this situation, you need to use the give skills first. The group needs to hear the impact of their behavior pattern and a clear statement of what you expect. The cycle has remained stuck as a result of you not giving them clear feedback (criticism) about their silence and clear expectations.

4. **Prepare a practice script. Pretend the person is in front of you. What is your opening statement?**

- "I'm concerned about the pattern of silence within this group when we are discussing an issue." (*Give feelings: acknowledge as a resource, own with "I".*)

- "When you don't speak up about your feelings and views on an issue, I can't make decisions that will be satisfactory to everyone or that are the best quality decisions. That means our service can suffer as a result and none of us in this department will look as credible as we could." (*Give criticism: describe behavior, clarify impact.*)

- "When we are discussing an issue that affects all of us, I need to be assured that I will hear from all of you at the time we are discussing it and even without my asking you specifically." (*Give expectations: clear focus, make assumptions explicit.*)

Imagine two different responses from the other person. Write the dialogue you could use to deal with these responses in a way that keeps the communication process going and builds respect.

One possible reponse from the group might be "Okay" (One or two nod in agreement).

This quick compliance with your request may be deceptive. They may be hoping you will just let it go. This is a good opportunity to use your take in skills to pursue what is meant.

Manager: "So you are saying then, that you are all in agreement with changing the ways in which you have participated in our meeting discussions?" (*Reflect content: interpret, tentative.*)

If they still agree, ask for suggestions from them about specific steps to take to change the process of the meetings so that everyone contributes to the discussion. Be prepared to wait out some silence. It may be helpful to ask them all to write down one idea individually about how to change the meeting discussion process. Then ask each person to read it out. This will signal that you are serious about addressing the issue and making some changes.

If they are silent after your initial "reflect content" statement, reiterate your focused expectation and go on to "Seek information" about what stops them from participating. (e.g., "What makes it difficult to give me your views…?" "How prepared do you feel to discuss the different items when they come up on the agenda…?")

Another possible response from the group might be, "But it doesn't matter what we think anyway."

This sounds like criticism of you or of the decision-making process in the organization as a whole. It is probably criticism that is worthwhile exploring for more. Note how quick your "gut reaction" is to answer "Yes it does!" If you do this you are basically discounting their input. It's more effective to acknowledge and take in their feedback than to deny, deflect, or discount it.

"What has given you the impression that it doesn't matter what you think?" (Take in criticism: explore for more.) If you have a long history with silence in this group, be prepared to wait it out after your questions. If your focus is clear for you and your intent is in line (you want to enhance the capacity of all concerned), you will find it easier to be patient. If your intent is to control them, make them do what you want because you want it, you will find it harder to wait without getting frustrated and impatient.

5. **Assess the script you have written. What might be the results for you? For the relationship? For the work itself?**

For you—you can benefit from increased self-esteem because you are dealing with an issue that has been undermining you. You and your staff will likely increase respect for each other because you are not easily side-tracked. The level of trust between you and your staff will also likely increase because you are defining and dealing with an issue which causes conflict between you. The quality of decisions could improve if all staff take the responsibility to participate.

d. YOUR TURN: YOU BE THE STAR PERFORMER

Worksheets #21 through #28 present a number of case scenarios. These scenarios represent real work situations described by managers just like yourself. In each situation, the manager felt stuck and kept using a reactive pattern — either passive or aggressive. Work through each one following the five worksheet questions.

If you need help, go back to the two dress rehearsal examples in order to clarify what the questions mean. You can also check with the suggested guidelines that follow the worksheets. The suggested guidelines are suggestions only. Clearly, there can be many different effective responses in each of the case situations by using a different combination of the basic assertive skills. In addition, each discussion would be longer than the few responses you are asked to create.

These worksheet questions are intended to help you understand how to get the unproductive pattern unstuck — how to get to first base and to prepare you for one or two of the responses you might get from the other person. These worksheets are not intended to provide you with a script to memorize. When you are clear and present, you don't need a memorized script. Remember, too, that the way you choose to deal with a work situation must take into account the three critical questions:

- What is your intent?
- Who's in charge?
- What are you creating?

e. GET TO FIRST BASE ON YOUR OWN WORK ISSUE

Use Worksheet #29 as an opportunity for you to apply what you've learned to a work situation of your own. Think about your interactions at work with clients, with your colleagues and coworkers, and with your staff. Where are the stuck, unproductive cycles? You may want to look at Worksheet #1 in chapter 1 where you first described several different situations in which you can't get to first base.

Use Worksheet #29 in the same way you worked on the other case scenario worksheets in this chapter. It is an opportunity to make sure your focus and intent are clear and a chance to think through how you might put the basic assertive skills to work for you. This worksheet is not intended to give you a script to memorize.

Mark is one of my assembly line supervisors. He is often unsure about the instructions he gives his workers, but does not take the time to ensure they are correct. Then, when an assembler — Pete, for example — performs a task incorrectly, Mark does nothing about it, saying to himself something like "It's no big deal. Anyway, Pete would get upset if I said anything." As a result, Mark's staff lose their respect for him, create errors that bog down the work for others, and don't improve their skills enough to be considered for promotion. I have been watching Mark's supervisory style and have decided to speak to him about my concerns.

1. Focus: What is your focus? Is this a pattern or single event?

_____

_____

_____

_____

2. What's at stake for you in this situation?

_____

_____

_____

_____

3. What does the situation need in order to get to first base? (Give skills/Take in skills)?

_____

_____

_____

_____

4. Prepare a practice script. Pretend the person is in front of you. What is your opening statement?

_____

_____

_____

_____

Imagine two different responses from the other person. Write the dialogue you could use to deal with these responses in a way that keeps the communication process going and building respect.

_____

_____

_____

_____

_____

_____

_____

_____

_____

_____

_____

5. Assess the script you have written, what might be the results — for you? for the relationship? for the work itself?

_____

_____

_____

_____

_____

_____

_____

_____

_____

_____

_____

_____

_____

I have an employee, Thomas, whom I don't see very frequently — about every three to four weeks — because I travel from office to office around the province. When I do see him, we agree on what needs to change and what action he'll take, but he doesn't follow through, saying things like "Don't worry, I'll get to it" or "Something came up." etc. How can I deal with the fact that he agrees but doesn't do and that I'm not there for day-to-day follow-up and encouragement.

1. Focus: What is your focus? Is this a pattern or single event?

_____

_____

_____

_____

2. What's at stake for you in this situation?

_____

_____

_____

_____

3. What does the situation need in order to get to first base? (Give skills/Take in skills)

_____

_____

_____

_____

4. Prepare a practice script. Pretend the person is in front of you. What is your opening statement?

_____

_____

_____

_____

Imagine two different responses from the other person. Write the dialogue you could use to deal with these responses in a way that keeps the communication process going and builds respect.

_____

_____

_____

_____

_____

_____

_____

_____

_____

_____

_____

5. Assess the script you have written, what might be the results — for you? for the relationship? for the work itself?

_____

_____

_____

_____

_____

_____

_____

_____

_____

_____

_____

_____

_____

_____

Jim, a new (but permanent) employee has been producing high quality work under my supervision. He has a wide range of technical skills and was hired as a specialist in computer analysis and data-base work. I have recently received unsolicited comments from some of the staff, criticizing his communication skills/style: "Is he slow or something?" "Has the cat got his tongue?" "He doesn't seem to be mixing and communicating well with his colleagues." Others are getting frustrated and ignoring him.

1. Focus. What is your focus? Is this a pattern or single event?

_____

_____

_____

_____

2. What's at stake for you in this situation?

_____

_____

_____

_____

3. What does the situation need in order to get to first base? (Give skills/Take in skills)

_____

_____

_____

_____

4. Prepare a practice script. Pretend the person is in front of you. What is your opening statement?

_____

_____

_____

_____

Imagine two different responses from the other person. Write the dialogue you could use to deal with these responses in a way that keeps the communication process going and builds respect.

_____

_____

_____

_____

_____

_____

_____

_____

_____

_____

5. Assess the script you have written, what might be the results — for you? for the relationship? for the work itself?

_____

_____

_____

_____

_____

_____

_____

_____

_____

_____

_____

_____

_____

_____

Joe joined my department two years ago as a draftsperson. He came with average recommendations, but I hired him anyway because I needed help desperately. I have been pleasantly surprised by his performance. Until recently, he worked hard and consistently produced high-quality work. I know he has the ability to do good work. However, during the past few months he has definitely slacked off. He doesn't seem as excited about his work and I have noticed him daydreaming several times at his desk. I have decided it is time to call him in to discuss my concerns. Joe is 35 years old. He has been a draftsman since graduating from tech school, right after high school. He is married and has four children. He has worked for three other firms in twelve years.

1. Focus: What is your focus? Is this a pattern or single event?

_____

_____

_____

_____

2. What's at stake for you in this situation?

_____

_____

_____

_____

3. What does the situation need in order to get to first base? (Give skills/Take in skills)

_____

_____

_____

_____

4. Prepare a practice script. Pretend the person is in front of you. What is your opening statement?

_____

_____

_____

_____

Imagine two different responses from the other person. Write the dialogue you could use to deal with these responses in a way that keeps the communication process going and builds respect.

_____

_____

_____

_____

_____

_____

_____

_____

_____

_____

_____

5. Assess the script you have written, what might be the results — for you? for the relationship? for the work itself?

_____

_____

_____

_____

_____

_____

_____

_____

_____

_____

_____

_____

_____

_____

One of my senior managers, Jackie, has the habit of speaking to me privately about important issues. She has excellent insight and good ideas; however, when I put one of the issues on the agenda for the managers' meetings, she remains silent. When she doesn't say anything, I finally do and it makes me look like I'm over-controlling. Besides, Jackie loses credibility and respect with her peers. Others lose out on valuable information and the issues don't really get addressed seriously.

1. Focus: What is your focus? Is this a pattern or single event?

_____

_____

_____

_____

2. What's at stake for you in this situation?

_____

_____

_____

_____

3. What does the situation need in order to get to first base? (Give skills/Take in skills)

_____

_____

_____

_____

4. Prepare a practice script. Pretend the person is in front of you. What is your opening statement?

_____

_____

_____

_____

_____

_____

Imagine two different responses from the other person. Write the dialogue you could use to deal with these responses in a way that keeps the communication process going and builds respect.

_____

_____

_____

_____

_____

_____

_____

_____

_____

_____

_____

5. Assess the script you have written, what might be the results — for you? for the relationship? for the work itself?

_____

_____

_____

_____

_____

_____

_____

_____

Humphrey is a tech specialist in my department who is unwilling to spend some time to help people correct errors in their work by sorting out difficulties. He exhibits sarcasm, arrogance, and disinterest in the problems of coworkers. When approached, he frequently responds to the question, "What about this?" with "Wrong." or "Go ahead. Try it." in a mocking superior tone. I have decided to speak to Humphrey about the lack of concern/support for other team members.

1. Focus: What is your focus? Is this a pattern or single event?

_____

_____

_____

_____

2. What's at stake for you in this situation?

_____

_____

_____

_____

3. What does the situation need in order to get to first base? (Give skills/Take in skills)

_____

_____

_____

_____

4. Prepare a practice script. Pretend the person is in front of you. What is your opening statement?

_____

_____

_____

_____

Imagine two different responses from the other person. Write the dialogue you could use to deal with these responses in a way that keeps the communication process going and builds respect.

_____

_____

_____

_____

_____

_____

_____

_____

_____

_____

_____

5. Assess the script you have written, what might be the results - for you? for the relationship? for the work itself?

_____

_____

_____

_____

_____

_____

_____

_____

_____

Gene is older than I am (I am a woman) and has been with the firm longer than I have, but I am in a more senior position than he is. He is as uncooperative as possible in performance and in providing information and help to others. He attempts to give the department — and me — a bad name, indulging in negative gossip about the projects we work on. I have decided to speak to him.

1. Focus: What is your focus? Is this a pattern or single event?

_____

_____

_____

_____

2. What's at stake for you in this situation?

_____

_____

_____

_____

3. What does the situation need in order to get to first base? (Give skills/Take in skills)

_____

_____

_____

_____

4. Prepare a practice script. Pretend the person is in front of you. What is your opening statement?

_____

_____

_____

_____

_____

_____

Imagine two different responses from the other person. Write the dialogue you could use to deal with these responses in a way that keeps the communication process going and builds respect.

_____

_____

_____

_____

_____

_____

_____

_____

_____

_____

5. Assess the script you have written, what might be the results — for you? for the relationship? for the work itself?

_____

_____

_____

_____

_____

_____

_____

_____

_____

_____

_____

_____

_____

Emily, a staff member, has mentioned that Ashley, a long-time employee, doesn't appear to be pulling her weight. Ashley has a strong dependable work record and is very popular and helpful to fellow staff. Upon observation, I find that, in fact, Ashley is gradually delegating her duties to other employees. I casually question her about this and she replies: "After all these years of hard, loyal service, if you feel this way then I have no choice but to resign."

1. Focus: What is your focus? Is this a pattern or single event?

_____

_____

_____

_____

2. What's at stake for you in this situation?

_____

_____

_____

_____

3. What does the situation need in order to get to first base? (Give skills/Take in skills)

_____

_____

_____

_____

4. Prepare a practice script. Pretend the person is in front of you. What is your opening statement?

_____

_____

_____

_____

_____

Imagine two different responses from the other person. Write the dialogue you could use to deal with these responses in a way that keeps the communication process going and builds respect.

_____

_____

_____

_____

_____

_____

_____

_____

_____

_____

_____

_____

_____

5. Assess the script you have written, what might be the results — for you? for the relationship? for the work itself?

_____

_____

_____

_____

_____

_____

_____

_____

_____

_____

_____

SUGGESTED GUIDELINES
CASE #1: MARK

1. Focus

Help Mark develop more confidence in his supervisory skills. Treat it as a pattern.

2. At stake

Being misunderstood. In my efforts to be supportive, I may be "too nice," not direct enough about how important I think this is.

Fear of not having an answer to his insecurities or questions. As a result, I may overcontrol the discussion to make sure he doesn't raise a concern that leaves me with nothing to say.

3. Situation needs

Give skills. Give my expectations re what I expect of my supervisors with respect to learning, pushing their own limits.

4. Opening statement

Manager: Mark, I wanted to talk with you today to make sure you understood what I'm expecting from you in your role as a supervisor. I want you to try things out with your staff in order for you to learn what you do with them that works really well and what you do that doesn't. And I'll support you as you learn that.

Possible response from Mark, "So what am I doing wrong?"

Manager: I'm not talking about right or wrong, Mark. I'm more interested in your learning. I want you to take more responsibility to try different supervisory skills with your crew even if you're not too comfortable with it. (*Give expectations. Don't let him take you off track onto the path of judgment and blame. Stay focused.*)

Mark: Well, it's hard. They're all my friends, you know!

Manager: So you're feeling a bit nervous about giving instructions or corrections to your friends." (*Reflect feelings: acknowledge, label.*) "When you don't give correct feedback on their work, they may continue producing poor quality products and that won't help them learn to be more effective for their own careers. (*Give criticism: describe behavior, clarify impact.*)

5. Results:

For you, pride in working on critical priority re development of staff. For the relationship, more trust. For the work itself, clearer expectations re work standards, work behavior.

CASE #2: THOMAS

1. Focus

Need to rely on Thomas to work in closer partnership with me. Pattern.

2. At stake

Fear losing control — and that seems to be what's happening. Don't want to overreact.

3. Situation needs

Give skills. Need to give Thomas criticism about the current pattern.

4. Opening statement

Manager: Thomas, I'm aware that on several occasions we have agreed to plans but you haven't carried them out as we had agreed. When you don't follow through on plans as we have discussed them, I feel let down and confused about what I can rely on with you at your office in the future. In addition, sometimes your office is not able to benefit from the coordinated effort of the whole company because you haven't completed certain parts of a project. (*Give criticism: describe behavior; clarify impact.*)

Possible response from Thomas: "Well don't worry, from now on I'll get to it."

Manager: Yes, I can appreciate that you intend to *(reflect content)*, but I am concerned that we establish a more effective way of working together so that I can rely on you. I need a better partnership with you so that either what we've agreed to is what you are doing or you are keeping in touch with me about possible adjustments to the original plan. *(Give expectations: clear focus, make assumptions explicit.)*

Thomas: How could I help it. It wasn't my fault Susan got sick last month and the computer went down.

Manager: Sounds like you think I want you to control the office so nothing unexpected ever happens. *(Reflect content: interpret, tentative. Be aware at this point that Thomas has taken you off your "pattern" focus and down to single event, i.e., "last month.")*

There will always be something unexpected that comes up. But what I need to work out with you now is how you and I can work in closer partnership, together, so that we are both aware of what's happening here and I can rely on you... *(Give expectations — back on track with your focus.)*

5. Results

For you, reduced frustration, less reactive to Thomas' style. For the relationship, increased respect. Work more as partners, less blame and justifying. For the work itself, clearer expectations. Could result in innovations in the system.

CASE #3: JIM

1. Focus

Help Jim develop more effective team player (interaction) skills. Pattern.

2. At stake

Feel insecure. Jim knows more than I do technically. I think he'll challenge the importance I put on team skills. I don't want to get defensive and start justifying.

3. Situation needs

Give skills. Give expectations. So far this situation has been stuck in an unproductive cycle because Jim has never heard this expectation so directly from me.

4. Opening statement

Manager: Jim, I believe in managing a department such as ours in ways that all members of the project group can learn from and support each other. No one's work is completely independent. I want to talk with you today about how you could take a more active role in communicating with some of the other staff. *(Give expectations: clear focus, make assumptions explicit.)*

Possible response from Jim: "I don't need anybody's help."

Manager: That may be so, technically. Nevertheless when you are reluctant to interact with and speak with the other staff, they don't get to know you well, you don't get to know them well, and that makes it more difficult to understand how we can best use the mix of talents here on different projects. *(Give criticism: Describe behavior, clarify impact.)* I think the way in which we learn about each other and the way we learn to work together has an impact on the quality of the projects designed in my department as a whole. *(Give opinion: Follow this with a short statement repeating your expectation.)*

Jim: I haven't got time to talk to people.

Manager: So then, what you're saying is that you don't see that interacting with others, speaking with them, is an important part of your role here. *(Reflect content: interpret, tentative.)*

If he argues that it's not part of his role, go back to your focus. As a manager, you have a responsibility to define expectations — including work style expectations. If he agrees that it is part of his role, move on in your discussion to discuss how he could best be a more effective team player until you get agreement on specific new steps or new behavior.

In one office, one of the steps taken for an employee in Jim's situation was to let him (and the other staff in turn) make a mini-presentation about one of his projects at the regular staff meeting. This gave him more visibility, legitimized a way for him to start communicating better, and gave others a chance to see him being effective.

5. Results

For you, decreased stress. Discomfort with others tells me about a problem I haven't had the courage to deal with. For the relationship, increased respect. We still may not agree with each other or like each other, but we are dealing with the issue. For the work itself, clearer expectations. Specific steps that he and I will agree on. Improved learning for all concerned.

CASE #4: JOE

1. Focus

Clarify Joe's career decisions and demonstrate my support for them. Pattern.

2. At stake

Fear of not having an answer (being able to "fix" him). Recognize my role is to support him through his own choices, not take responsibility for his decisions.

3. Situation needs

Take in skills. Cycle has been stuck because I have been giving him encouragement, task assignments, and sometimes criticism without acknowledging and legitimizing what's going on with him.

4. Opening statement

Manager: Joe, one of the things I've been aware of for a while is that you seem to be reluctant to get involved in your work projects, even distracted at times, and that's a worry to me. *(Reflect feelings: label, tentative.)* I think it's important that people get something out of their work, that it pays off for you. *(Give opinion: own it with "I.")*

Possible response from Joe: "But my work's okay, isn't it?"

Manager: Joe, I'm less worried about the quality of your work right now than the fact that you don't seem to like it anymore. *(Reflect feelings: sometimes you need to reinforce the fact that it's okay for the other person to deal with the real issue.)*

Joe: I don't see any way to do anything different.

Manager: So then, are you saying you'd be interested in tackling something different if we could create it here? *(Reflect content: interpret, tentative.)* If Joe agrees, move on in the discussion to let him help you define what would be challenging to him. If he doesn't agree, seek information, e.g., "What is it that's causing you to feel turned off?"

5. Results

For you, satisfaction with demonstrating care. Increased self-esteem. For the relationship, less distance. More trust. Better understanding. Clear responsibilities. For the work itself, linking work style to quality. Possibility of creating enrichment options.

CASE #5: JACKIE

1. Focus

To have Jackie take more ownership/responsibility of her ideas. Pattern.

2. At stake

Scared I'll lose Jackie's ideas altogether if she feels pressured. Cycle has stayed stuck because I've compromised Jackie's development in order to make sure I got the ideas from her. Short-term perspective.

3. Situation needs

Give skills: Give expectations re her level of responsibility for her own ideas.

4. Opening statement

Manager: Jackie, I'd like you to take more responsibility for speaking about your own ideas in our staff and project meetings, rather than relying on me to do it based on discussions we have before the meeting. *(Give expectations: focus is clear, assumptions explicit.)*

Possible response from Jackie: "I don't like speaking up at meetings and, besides, isn't it more important that you have the information?"

Manager: Seems like you don't feel very comfortable in front of the group. *(Reflect feeling: Label, tentative.)* When you aren't willing to discuss your own ideas with the rest of the staff, they don't have the opportunity to recognize and credit the kind of work you do. This can make it more difficult for you later if you move into a project leader role. *(Give criticism: describe behavior, clarify impact.)*

Jackie: But you say it better than I would. They'll listen to you.

Manager: That may be so for now. Nevertheless, I don't think it's appropriate for me to take charge of what has rightfully been your research. *(Give opinion: own it. Follow with repeating your focused expectation in order to get back on track. Then move on to explore ways Jackie could learn to feel more comfortable. Your bottom line —that she start to take more ownership — is nonnegotiable. Your role is to help her learn how to do this.)*

5. Results

For you, less frustrated, more clear about my role. Not taking on responsibility inappropriately. For the relationship, more trust and respect. Clearer expectations. For the work itself, other staff more likely to participate in discussion on an issue if I'm not controlling. More resources; better ideas.

CASE #6: HUMPHREY

1. Focus

To have Humphrey see that one of his roles is to help other staff learn. Pattern.

2. At stake

Fear of being challenged by staff member who knows more than I do technically. What if he quits? Or criticizes me in the same sarcastic manner? Cycle has been stuck because I'm scared he'll turn his arrogant, intimidating style on me. Will I have the "right" answer?

3. Situation needs

Give skills: I need to be able to give criticism to Humphrey in a more effective way.

4. Opening statement:

Manager: When you are unwilling to take time to answer questions or give more complete instructions to other staff, they don't improve their own skills and our projects overall can lose out on quality. (*Give criticism: describe behavior, clarify impact.*)

Possible response from Humphrey: "They should know what they're doing."

Manager: That may be so. (*Take in criticism: don't challenge the irrelevant.*) Nevertheless, when you are unwilling to take time to help improve their understanding, our whole department loses the benefit of your and their expertise. (*Give criticism: repeat your main issue until he recognizes you are serious about it.*)

Humphrey: You should have hired better people.

If you choose to handle this as irrelevant criticism, see your above response. If you choose to handle this as relevant criticism, you can try the following in order to explore for more.

Manager: What is it about the abilities of the people I've hired that concerns you most? (*Take in criticism: explore for more.*)

If he has some valid observations for you, great, you can pursue it but don't let this take you off track from how you are expecting him to change his style. It's even more critical. If he has no valid observations for you, then you know his comment was basically an evasive tactic to get the focus off himself. Get back on track with a direct request to explore ways he could assist other staff more effectively.

5. Results

For you, decreased stress. Less fear of his intimidating style. Happy I could state a clear focus. For the relationship, more respect. He'll know I am serious and that I care about what's happening for all the staff and the projects. For the work itself, possibility of improved skill levels, better quality.

CASE #7: GENE

1. Focus

Concern about my relationship with Gene — need to be able to rely on his support.

2. At stake

Fear of having my authority/status challenged. Fear of not being liked by Gene. Competition — his, more than mine, as he probably resents my getting the job. I'm not in competition with him but I'm scared of being judged by him — am I managing okay??

3. Situation needs

Give skills. Give my expectations re quality of working relationship I want with him.

4. Opening statement

Manager: Gene, I need you more on my side in this department. I need to be able to rely on you to work with me in supporting the work in this department — in giving help to others and in how you talk about our projects to others outside the department. (*Give expectations: clear focus, make assumptions explicit.*) At this time I feel disappointed because I don't have that kind of working relationship with you and that concerns me. (*Give feelings: acknowledge, own with "I."*)

Possible response from Gene: "The last manager never complained about me. We got along just fine."

Manager: That may be so. (*Take in criticism: don't challenge the irrelevant.*) Nevertheless, I'm working with you now, and I'd like

122

to talk with you about how we could work better together so that I can rely more on your support. (*Give expectations: get back on track after irrelevant criticism.*)

Gene: So tell me *exactly* what you want me to do (very sarcastic tone)

Manager: Gene, even now, when you say that, you seem to imply that I am the only one who has responsibility to make the relationship between us work. Is that what your statement meant? (*Reflect content: interpret, tentative.*)

When a person with whom you have an issue at stake demonstrates that issue in front of you in the discussion, using that incident to "name it" is a very powerful way to help him or her see.

If Gene says, "Yes, you're the manager..." return to your focus and expectation. "Yes, that's true, but my definition of managing means that I look for ways to work with my staff in the most positive and effective way possible. I don't think we're doing that right now."

If Gene accepts your point and is willing to take some responsibility, go on to explore ways you can work better together until you agree on some specific steps.

5. Results

For you, higher self-esteem. Pride in sticking to my intention to develop myself as well as Gene. For the relationship, more respect. Clearer expectations. For work itself, specific steps to improve quality of information available.

CASE #8: ASHLEY

1. Focus

To agree on Ashley's role and responsibilities with her.

2. At stake

Fear of losing control of what's happening in the department. I might get too directive. Fear of upsetting Ashley — don't want her to think I don't like her, don't value her, want her to like me, and know I appreciate her. Don't know how to deal with her defensive reaction. Cycle stays stuck.

3. Situation needs

Take in skills. Give compliment to demonstrate I recognize and value her worth.

4. Opening statement

Manager: Ashley, you are now and have been one of the most valuable staff members in this department. Over the years you have consistently looked for ways to help other people learn new things and become more experienced. (*Give compliments: describe behavior, clarify impact.*) I wanted to talk with you today again because I felt distressed at your comment last week implying that I didn't value your service here. (*Give feeling: own with "I," acknowledge as a resource.*)

Possible response from Ashley: "So what's wrong with me now?"

Manager: When you delegate some of your work to others, I am not sure any more, and neither are some of the others, what you actually are accountable for. Sometimes the work isn't done properly simply because people didn't know whose work it was. (*Give criticism: describe behavior, clarify impact.*) You and I need to agree on what your role looks like now, particularly if you see it changing. (*Give expectations: focus is clear, make assumptions explicit.*)

Ashley: I want others to learn more about my work so they can do it when I retire.

Manager: You mean you've been working on a plan to get them ready to take over? (*Reflect content: interpret, tentative.*) If Ashley agrees, return to your focused expectation, elaborating on the fact that you and she need agreement on what that looks like.

In one office, this was exactly the case. The "Ashley" employee had taken it upon herself to initiate a career development plan for other staff without the manager's knowing. As a result of their discussion, Ashley and the manager worked more closely together beginning with redefining Ashley's role to include more training.

5. Results

For you, satisfaction in successfully demonstrating care. For the relationship, increased trust, affirmed liking, support, more enthusiasm. For work itself, enhanced capacities of all concerned, more skills, knowledge available in staff. Better quality service to clients.

Chapter 8 reading list

Cava, Roberta. *Difficult People: How to Deal with Impossible Clients, Bosses and Employees.* Toronto: Key Porter Books Limited, 1990.

Schaef, Anne Wilson and Diane Fassel. *The Addictive Organization: Why We Overwork, Cover up, Pick Up the Pieces, Please the Boss, and Perpetuate Sick Organizations.* San Francisco: Harper & Row, 1988.

Senge, Peter M. *The Fifth Discipline: The Art and Practice of the Learning Organization.* New York: Doubleday/Currency, 1990.

WORKSHEET #29
GETTING TO FIRST BASE

1. Describe a situation at work in which you feel blocked, stuck, repeating old patterns, can't get to first base.... Choose something fairly straightforward, not necessarily the biggest issue you have at work. For example, giving/receiving negative information, giving/receiving instructions or requests, trying to get more information, etc....

_____

_____

_____

_____

_____

_____

_____

_____

2. When this happens, what is the result:

For you?

_____

_____

For your relationship with the other person?

_____

_____

For the work itself?

_____

_____

_____

3. What's your focus? Is this a pattern or single event?

_____

_____

_____

4. What's at stake for you?

_____

_____

_____

_____

_____

_____

_____

5. What does this situation need in order for you to "get to first base"? Do you need to give something more effectively? Do you need to take in something more effectively?

_____

_____

_____

_____

_____

_____

6. Prepare a practice script. Pretend the person is in front of you. What is your opening statement?

_____

_____

_____

_____

_____

_____

_____

_____

_____

Imagine two different responses from the other person. Write the dialogue you could use to deal with these responses in a way that keeps the communication process going and builds respect.

_____

_____

_____

_____

_____

_____

_____

_____

_____

_____

7. Assess the script you have written. What might be the result?
For you?

_____

_____

For your relationship with the other person?

_____

_____

For the work itself?

_____

_____

_____

_____

_____

9

MAKING THE BREAKS:
ASSERTIVE SKILLS FOR WOMEN AT WORK

a. DO YOU RECOGNIZE YOURSELF?

Example #1

Helen worked hard to make sure her evenings were free of work concerns so that she could concentrate on the night school course she was taking in personnel management. She often skipped lunches to finish work at her desk, avoided others, and successfully minimized interruptions so that she could keep on top of her work. She was very keen to make a change from the accounting department into the human resources department. In fact, from her experiences in accounting, she had some good ideas about how the staff could be trained on the new computers. Since she couldn't move any higher in accounting either, she was sure that a transfer over to human resources would let her start moving up the management track. No one knew about her plans yet, but she felt sure she'd have a good chance once she got her diploma in personnel management.

Imagine her surprise — and dismay — one morning when Suzanne, a colleague of hers in accounting, announced that she'd been selected to transfer into human resources as the new management trainee. Suzanne, thought Helen, but how could they? I know more than she does already.

Example #2

Aleeta is one of the top performers in the word processing center. She caught on quickly to the new computer equipment. She could deal with the staff from other departments well even though they gave her projects with unclear instructions. She initiated a new system to record the priorities of the incoming projects so that the schedule would be fair and important projects would not be in danger of being put aside. Yet, when people tell her how much they appreciate her work, she often says "Oh, anybody could have done it. It's the computer that does it you know, not me. I still make a lot of mistakes."

Example #3

Bev, in charge of the financial resources for a large charity organization, went to her manager to talk about her ideas for the new fundraising campaign program she was developing for the next year. Her group had already made a number of attempts to solve a particular problem. Bev had some other alternatives that she wanted to explore but Bev's manager, who prided himself on his expert knowledge and superior insight, quickly took over the discussion. He told her how he would solve the problem in short order. Bev found herself unable to explain what the group had already tried. When her manager interrupted her and ignored her attempts to describe the issue, Bev simply nodded, listened half-heartedly to his "expert" advice and left feeling frustrated and annoyed.

All three women in the above example, Helen, Aleeta, and Bev, would be described by most as "good" employees: they're talented, they're conscientious, they're responsible. And they're all losing out. They can blame it on luck. (She got the breaks.) They can blame it on personality. (That's just the way I am.) They can blame it on a bad manager. (No one can work with him.) They can choose to live with the dissatisfaction and loss of motivation that result. Or, they can start to use assertive skills with a measure of political savvy to make sure they create more satisfying results for themselves.

You, too, can choose to use assertive skills to get people on your side, get recognized and valued for what you do, and handle intimidating tactics from others that block your efforts.

As described in chapter 1, the changes in the workplace and in society's attitudes and values have created a lot of pressure on managers. Women, whether managers or not, are often increasingly affected by these changes. You do have more options now. Different life styles and job styles have been legitimized. Computerization, dual-career families, job sharing, greater advancement opportunities, and nontraditional career opportunities all put an extra demand on your assertive skills: to decide, to justify, and to explain your choice.

In addition to the pressures to take charge of their choices, women are often also faced with an "implementation" problem. You, along with many other women, have already got a lot of the knowledge and information you need from your personal history, experience, training, and education. Where women lose out is in implementing that knowledge — making what you know work for you.

Your technical or professional development can stagnate when you lack the basic assertive skills to integrate your work with others.

"I'm the best C.A. here but I still don't get the good projects."

"She just doesn't have the team on her side."

Your career planning may falter when you can't implement the knowledge you have about your skills or available options because you lack the assertive skills to initiate the first step.

"I don't like talking about myself."

"He probably won't want to tell me about his job."

Even though you have a lot of knowledge about good leadership or effective problem solving (delegation, goal setting, etc.), you may fail to inspire others because you lack the assertive skills to implement your knowledge effectively. You sit in silence while someone steals your ideas.

"I can't get my staff to meet the deadlines we agreed on. They just won't cooperate."

How you use assertive skills affects all people in all disciplines at all levels in any size organization. You need to understand and become competent in the basic assertive skills described in the earlier chapters. But more than that, to make your knowledge and training work for you, you need to know how to use these basic skills to manage the political and power dynamics that run through all organizations.

The political and power dynamics include the following:

- Networking: getting people on your side and you on theirs

- Visibility: getting recognized and valued for what you do

- Managing intimidation: getting around the blocks that undermine your efforts.

You may survive in organizations without managing these three issues well, but you can't flourish. The discussion and exercises that follow will help you learn how to manage these three issues effectively.

When you can use assertive skills to manage networking, visibility, and intimidation, you will have solved the implementation problem and be on your way to making the breaks for yourself.

b. NETWORKING

1. Why network?

Think about what networking can do for you, your organization, or your profession.

Try Worksheet #30 to see how often and why you network.

(a) Increase available information

Effective networking builds an image for you, your firm, or your profession. Who and how many people know you and know what you do? Who and how many people do you know? Do you know who knows whom? Do you know what's going on in your organization? Getting information is even more difficult now with the trend toward computerization. There may be more information available but it may often be known by people who aren't in the traditional upward/downward communication channels.

Better information about you and for you will improve your perceptions, decisions, and actions. In the example at the beginning of this chapter, Helen didn't know what her organization wanted as preparation for a transfer into human resources. She made assumptions, and lost. Also, appropriate people did not know about Helen's intentions. Helen would have been smart to use her basic assertive skills to give information to others, seek information from others, share her feelings about her current situation and anticipated plans, and give her expectations.

(b) Build trust

This intangible factor — sometimes referred to as integrity, new age ethics, age of commitment — is surfacing more and more frequently in media reports and popular books about organizational life. Other things being equal (technical skills, fees, education, etc.), clients often hire professionals on the basis of trust, and key decision makers in organizations often promote, transfer, or assign special projects to people on the basis of trust.

Trust is not elusive. Trust can be deliberately generated and nurtured through networking. When you are actively building alliances, people have the opportunity to assess your competencies — to see your strengths

WORKSHEET #30
HOW WELL DO YOU NETWORK?

For each statement below, put an X toward the end of the continuum that comes closest to your situation.

I can initiate conversation with people I don't know at work.

NEVER _____ALL THE TIME

I keep in touch with those in my network even when I don't need anything.

NEVER _____ALL THE TIME

When I need something (help, information, etc.), I can ask for it clearly.

NEVER _____ALL THE TIME

and weaknesses. This builds trust. When you are building good alliances you are also taking the time to work through any differences in opinions or attitudes.

Helen wasn't aware that she could trust others with her ambitions. She also has not handled her interactions with others in ways that give them the opportunity to know her — and trust her. Helen could have used the basic assertive skills of give and take in to demonstrate her competencies and work through any differences.

(c) Manage interdependence

Nowadays, many people affect your performance. The quality of the final outcome of your job and your organization's product or service is affected by mutual respect and collaboration among a diverse and complex network of colleagues, support people, clients, professional and personal contacts, and financial community, the media, etc. Few are exempt from the growing interdependence in our organizational life.

Effective networking builds a better, more varied resource base. This base works both ways. People can collaborate with you. You can help them.

Helen appears to be independent to an extreme. She is not doing her part to generate the kind of give and take that makes individuals and organizations effective. She may have finished her course, but she lost her opportunity. As well, the organization may have lost (and never known about) an opportunity to use their human resources with more flexibility and creativity.

(d) Increase personal well-being and career success

Studies have shown that one of the two main sources of well-being for women is the number and quality of their "arenas for intimacy" (alliances or relationships with others).*

Many women find that they are relying on only one or two people in their network. This is not only unrealistic, it is potentially dangerous. If the relationship should end, they may find themselves without any allies.

Increase the numbers and diversity in your network. Use your assertive skills to build alliances with those above, beside, and below you, with those in other functions and departments, both inside and outside your organization. Studies have indicated that one of the critical factors contributing to career success is sensitivity to your impact on others.** Many women make assumptions about how others perceive them — but lack the assertive skills to check out these assumptions.

Helen blocked access to others by avoiding lunch, socializing, and interruptions too much. She may have gained time at the expense of her own well-being. Helen would have been smart to use some of her time and her basic assertive skills to include others instead of setting up barriers.

2. Use the basic assertive skills to network better

In Worksheets #31 to #34 you'll find some situations described that are common to most of us. You can use these to learn how to use assertive skills to build better relationships in your network.

In the space given in each worksheet, write in what you would normally say. Don't worry about trying to be right. Just write down your first response. If the situation has never happened to you, use your imagination to make it as realistic as you can.

Check your responses against the examples that follow each worksheet. Use the key tips for using assertive skills to network to practice and improve your own responses.

---

*(See *Life Prints: New Patterns of Love and Work for Today's Woman* by Grace Baruch, et al. New American Library, 1983.)

**(See "Why Fast-Trackers Derail" by Henry Weil in *SAVVY Magazine*, January, 1984.)

WORKSHEET #31
WHAT DO YOU DO?

You have just sat down next to another person at a meeting (conference, night school class, lunch table, etc.). After a brief exchange of names, she asks, "What do you do?"

You say:

_____

_____

_____

_____

_____

_____

Check your response. Use assertive skills to network better.

> I'm currently working on a new health records system so we can respond faster to school outbreaks — like the measles outbreak that just happened. (NOT: "I'm a public health nurse.")

> Our tax department is being computerized and I'm right in the middle of training some of the staff on the new equipment. (NOT: "I'm an accountant.")

KEY TIPS

Remember the basic assertive skill of giving information. You can use it here to build better alliances.

- **Describe yourself in action** — Paint a verbal picture of yourself in action. It doesn't have to be your whole job description. Choose a current issue, in-terest, project, etc. Provide details, action words, impact for others. Using only your job title (records clerk, receptionist, secretary) labels you and gives your listener nowhere to go next in the conversation. Sure, they can ask you — but why should they do all the work? Remember, you are responsible for keeping the communication process going and for building mutual respect by the way you give information.

  If you are too general, (e.g., "I'm in accounting") you leave too much interpretation up to the listener. Some listeners may not know how or may not want to pursue it. ("Oh, I guess she doesn't want to talk about it." "I don't know much about that and I don't know what to ask.")

- **Be direct; no bias or judgment** — Just the straight facts. No overtones or undertones of bias or judgment. Allow your listener to come back into the discussion without you directing what they should think or feel about your job. It's hard to respond to someone who says, "Oh, I just hate what I'm doing now..." or "I'm only a receptionist...."

Naturally there are times when you don't want to or it's not appropriate to give information about what you do.

Most of us already know a lot of ways to close down the conversation and the connection. Do you know how to respond assertively to open doors for yourself?

Now check your response again. Is it descriptive and direct? In Worksheet #32, rewrite your response choosing two different ways you can describe your current activities.

WORKSHEET #32
WHAT DO YOU DO? REWRITE

1. _____

_____

_____

_____

_____

_____

2. _____

_____

_____

_____

_____

Your friend, Val, has an excellent reputation for writing effective resumes and using good job search techniques. You are trying to make a career change and know she could help you with some excellent tips. You decide to call and ask her.

You say:

_____

_____

_____

_____

_____

_____

_____

Check your response. Use assertive skills to network better.

> Val, I'd appreciate it if you would look at two different drafts of my new resume to tell me which has more impact. Will you have time to look at them this week?

> Val, I'd like to get your opinion on the kinds of questions I'm going to ask my contacts about the job area I'm investigating. Could I bring them with me when we meet for coffee tomorrow?

KEY TIPS

Remember the basic assertive skills to state your needs. You can use this skill to build better alliances.

- **Be specific** — Focus clearly on what it is you really want or need. A general-

ized, all-encompassing plea for help won't work. Your ally — or potential ally — often doesn't know where to begin for you and may not support you in the way you hope simply because she feels unsure or overwhelmed. Not wanting to appear incompetent, she may respond with "I'm really tied up right now…I'm not sure I'm going to have time." (Would you want to start from square one with someone else's resume if that person hadn't done his or her homework on it first?) Being specific helps your ally feel and be effective, and you develop better networking relationships.

- **Invite reactions** — Make it easy for your ally to respond to your request or expectation. This is particularly important if your request is followed by silence. Many women fall into the trap of immediately thinking "Oh, I shouldn't have asked…she doesn't want to do it…she's too busy…." Help your ally respond by inviting reactions along any one of a number of directions: timing, obstacles of problems in the way, ability to meet your needs, willingness to meet your needs, etc.

- **Claim your right to ask** — You have a right to ask for help, advice, information, assistance, opinions, etc. If you do not grant yourself that right, no one else will respect it (or you) either. Don't undermine yourself by adding on tag beginnings or endings that sound like: "You may not have time…." "I'm sorry to have to ask you this…." "…if it's all right with you…." Many women make assumptions about someone else's limits: too busy, too important, not interested, doesn't like me, etc. Don't give up your right to ask, for fear of the consequences; learn, instead, to deal with them.

Check your response to the previous situation. Is it specific? Do you invite reactions? Do you claim your right to ask without undermining yourself or apologizing? In Worksheet #34, rewrite your response choosing two different specific needs.

You have a right to ask for help

WORKSHEET #34
ASKING FOR HELP REWRITE

1. _____

_____

_____

_____

2. _____

_____

_____

_____

3. What's stopping you?

What's stopping you from using basic assertive skills to network better? Which of the following arguments do you find yourself using?

- **I haven't got time; I'm too busy** — Is procrastination an issue for you? Some women put off using new skills without realizing that procrastination can be a form of protection from anything novel or risky. How does not changing serve you? For some, it may protect against failure; for others it may protect against success.

  People successful in their careers don't network only if there is time, or by accident, or if it's convenient. Doing your job well and waiting to be noticed won't work. Successful people spend part of their work time reaching out to build contacts and alliances and to project the potential of their abilities and/or their organization's services or products.

- **I'm too shy. I can't talk to people I don't know well** — Is possible rejection an issue for you? The need to be liked may interfere with your willingness to try new skills to build better alliances. It is helpful to separate "liking" from "respect." Focus on building respect, which is one of the goals of assertive skills. Respect is based on clear, descriptive, non-judgmental, two-way interaction. The basic assertive skills described in this book will help you do this. Liking may follow as an outcome, but it is often not a viable goal in working relationships.

- **I already have enough contacts/friends** — Networking is not direct, one-for-one reciprocation. You should be networking because richer relationships are a better way to be and feel effective, not because **you** need something. Think of it as planting seeds for future possibilities. Even if no career benefit arises, the relationship is a valued goal itself. Remember that your sense of well-being (self-esteem) depends on the number, depth, and variety of your alliances. Trace a map of any one of your current achievements or projects to discover how unforeseen — and unlikely — some of the connections were.

- **I don't know how (I'm not perfect yet)** — Are you a perfectionist? For some women, "being perfect" actually reflects a need to control everything. Effective networking cannot be controlled by one side, nor can it be perfect. Effective networking implies continuous change and development with movement and energy from both sides. Think of yourself as a learner/explorer rather than an expert. Let go of control in order to start the process. Recognize that you cannot control the outcome either, but you can learn to deal with the ongoing consequences as they arise by developing competent assertive skills.

c. GAINING VISIBILITY

Many women think it is enough just to do a good job and don't realize that the visibility of their work affects their success, the success of their projects, and the successful collaborative links with other people or projects in other departments. Of course, using assertive skills to build better alliances will lead to increased visibility. However, there are some specific skills to use with your alliances to make sure visibility works for you.

It is your responsibility to know how to "set up images" of your work in such a way that others can recognize and value what you do. Setting up images means giving information about your skills and your work and the impact that your work has on others. Others need to know how to interpret what you do. This may involve, for example, giving opinions, taking in compliments, and giving or seeking information. Try Worksheet #35 to see how visible you are at work

For each statement below, put an X toward the end of the continuum that comes closest to your situation.

I can accept valid compliments from others without feeling uncomfortable.

NEVER _____ALL THE TIME

I can give a clear, descriptive statement of what I contribute at work.

NEVER _____ALL THE TIME

I can give my opinion in a meeting without feeling uncomfortable.

NEVER _____ALL THE TIME

1. What should be visible?

Use assertive skills to gain visibility in two different areas: you and your job activities.

(a) You need to be visible

Others need to know more about your skills, special talents, interests, past experience, current contributions. Don't make assumptions that it isn't relevant, isn't appropriate, doesn't count or isn't good enough. One example is Judy, who helps coordinate regional volleyball tournaments since she's not playing competitively herself anymore. When her accounting firm wanted to include team games in an annual retreat, Judy was asked to coordinate the committee to set up the scheduling. In this role she got to work with people from offices across the country.

(b) Your job activities need to be visible

Others need to know what your job activities are, particularly if you are working on any committees, special assignments, task forces, new trends, etc. They also need to know about those job activities that are autonomous and relevant. Any job activity that lets you be in charge, make decisions, set schedules, and holds you accountable for errors is an "autonomous job activity." Any job activity that is related to the core issues or key problems of the department or organization is a "relevant job activity."

When you think about these job activities, think in terms of the impact your work has for others and in terms of what role you play. This is strictly information, not boasting. There is a fine line between the two, which often depends on your body language and tone of voice. However, as a general rule, the more descriptive the information, the better.

Compare the following:

I just changed the whole line-up for the word processing project. (Too boastful.)

vs.

When I was working out a new system for setting priorities for the word processing projects, I was amazed to discover how different the needs are in the different departments. (Better description.)

Compare:

What a job. I hope everybody appreciates what I did to get everyone to finally agree at that meeting. (Demanding recognition won't work with others.)

vs.

I just had a very tough meeting — but successful — with the other managers trying to get them to agree to us going ahead with the project. (Providing information and impact works better.)

Increased visibility means increased power. When other people can recognize and value your special skills, talents, job involvement, and impact on them or others, they are more likely to see where you fit in, and, therefore, where you matter.

In addition, increased visibility makes it easier for others to know where they can connect or collaborate with you or your job.

2. Use the basic assertive skills to increase visibility

In Worksheets #36 to #39, write your own response to the situations described, then read the examples and discussion. Check your response and use the key tips for assertive skills to improve your response.

Gaining visibility

138

WORKSHEET #36
ACCEPTING COMPLIMENTS

A coworker has just complimented you on your fine presentation at the staff meeting. "Good work, Sandy. I really like the way you handled Ted and Julie with the sarcastic comments. You didn't let them take over."

You say:

_____

_____

_____

_____

_____

_____

_____

Check your response. Use assertiveness skills to gain visibility.

> Thanks. I like hearing that. I do feel more comfortable handling the objectors now.

> Thank you. I appreciate the comment.

KEY TIPS

Remember the basic assertive skill to take in compliments? You can use it here to gain visibility.

- **Acknowledge the other person's input —** Value the compliment without evaluation. Should you judge a compliment? There are many ways to acknowledge someone's input: a smile, a nod, direct eye contact, relaxed body posture to let it soak in. Check your comfort level with compliments. Does your own self-consciousness make you lose eye contact, brush it off, or judge whether they should have given you the credit?

- **Credit yourself —** "Oh, no...I didn't do anything." "Oh, it wasn't much." "Oh, it wasn't me." Sound familiar? Do you deny, discount, deflect compliments from others? When you do, you lose the esteem-building credit that you need for yourself to be able to do effective work. But, perhaps worse, you undermine the source.

When you devalue or discount someone's input, that person is not likely to try again.

Claim credit where credit is due you. A simple "Yes, I'm pleased with it, too," or "Thanks. I'm glad it was helpful to you" will do.

- **Pursue perceptions** — "Thanks. I like what you're saying but I'm not sure what you mean. Could you tell me more about what you saw happening...?" The danger when you don't know what the person means by the compliment is to take it fast and run away. Now you don't have information you can use about your impact on others, and the other person knows by your actions that you either didn't understand or didn't care. Take time to check it out. You gain information and visibility. "Great, but what did I do that was helpful?"

Now check your response again. In Worksheet #37, rewrite it showing how you can use assertive skills to acknowledge others, claim credit, and pursue perceptions.

WORKSHEET #37
ACCEPTING COMPLIMENTS REWRITE

140

During a job interview, the interviewer asks you, "Is there anything else we should know about you that we haven't asked?"

You say:

_____

_____

_____

_____

_____

_____

Check your response. Use assertive skills to gain visibility.

> I'm an amateur photographer and will be showing my work for the first time in late August as part of a community competition.

> In my last job, I could see a better way of organizing the hundreds of orders we'd get each week. When I prepared my plan and presented it to my manager she put me in charge of carrying out the project. Now other departments are asking about our system.

> I love baking and decorating special cakes. In fact, now I take orders from friends and family for wedding and special occasion cakes.

KEY TIPS

- **Describe yourself in action** — Learn to paint a verbal picture of yourself doing things: "showing my work," "prepared and presented," "love baking and decorating." Use action to describe your current job activities in progress. People who are successful in their careers know how to talk about work in progress. Women, in particular, often feel uncomfortable talking about themselves in action. Women have been more conditioned to be sensitive to and comment on or support other people's actions.

- **Describe impact for yourself or others** — Give specific examples of what happened for you as a result of your activities. How could you change the way you gave information about yourself and these activities to increase your visibility by describing action and impact?

Check your response to the previous situation. In Worksheet #39, rewrite your response to describe yourself in action and clarify the impact on yourself or others.

3. What's stopping you?

What's stopping you from using basic assertive skills to gain visibility? Which of the following arguments do you give yourself?

141

- **I'm just ordinary...nothing special about me** — Do you have trouble affirming your own unique set of talents, views, feelings, and experiences? Many people do — especially women. Think about your special achievements in more detail. When will you judge yourself as okay?

- **But I'm not very good at....** — Are you more in touch with what you can't do, what you're not good at or where you made mistakes? Everybody's not very good at something. Increasing your visibility means letting people see you as a whole person with a unique combination of abilities, feelings, and views. Focus on what you can do and have achieved rather than on what you can't do. it is this positive focus that builds self-esteem.

Include internal visibility as one part of increasing your visibility. Visualize yourself as successful. Expect to be successful at asserting yourself. See yourself taking credit for your accomplishments, acknowledging compliments as though you, too, believe you did well, giving opinions and views as though you, too, believe they matter.

Sit back and relax, close your eyes and see yourself talking and acting assertively. Visualize it happening, followed by a positive affirmation to yourself, such as —

"I have a right to say what I think."

"I will have better working relationships because I am more assertive."

"When I give my views, I am helping others."

d. MANAGING INTIMIDATION

How well do you manage intimidation? try Worksheet #40 to see when and how often you are able to deal with intimidation.

Remember Bev from the introduction to this chapter? Bev could not manage the intimidation from her boss. Bev has emotionally and mentally disappeared. She deferred to her boss's judgment of her work and of her, withdrew, and sacrificed her own self-respect and the respect of her boss.

Bev, like many other women, hasn't yet clearly affirmed to herself why she should learn to deal with criticism and intimidation. It isn't a high priority for her. It's stressful, but not yet enough of a priority for her personally to deal with the real issue. She reacts by withdrawing and deferring. This is a passive response. Others may react aggressively by attacking. Both are defensive styles and equally ineffective.

WORKSHEET #39
GAINING VISIBILITY REWRITE

_____

_____

_____

_____

_____

Unfortunately, the hostility and anger that gets generated inside Bev does not disappear. She feels angry at her boss for the way he treats her. She feels angry at herself for not being able to handle his intimidation. Bev takes this anger home, feeling depressed and drained of energy. If this pattern continues, she may start to question her own abilities and worth and experience lower self-esteem. Bev needs to use her basic assertive skills to manage this kind of intimidation and criticism to preserve her own self-esteem. This is the first priority. She may, with new skills, also solve the problem in a more creative way and/or influence a change in her boss's manner.

1. Criticism vs. intimidation

Bev, like many other women, has not made a clear distinction between criticism and intimidation. Both criticism and intimidation include what is said (the content) and how it is said (the process). With criticism the content is relevant; it is the information you need to learn how to change, modify, adjust, or improve your behavior. The process is irrelevant. Sometimes the information may be given to you in a way that is too loud, too public, too judgmental, or too long. But if you focus on the content, you will deal with the criticism in a way that benefits you, your job, and your relationship.

If Bev's boss had accused her with "That'll never work," Bev could have focused on the content and asked: "What is it about the plan that you think won't work...?" (Ignoring his obnoxious tone and valuing the content.)

With intimidation the process is relevant and critical. Aggressiveness, sarcasm, and cynicism, etc., are used to manipulate you. The actual content is irrelevant. A person intent on manipulating you through power is often not even aware of what words he or she is using. If you learn to respond to the process only — not the content — you will have a better chance of maintaining your self-respect and control of your own actions.

WORKSHEET #40
HOW WELL DO YOU HANDLE INTIMIDATION?

For each statement below, put an X toward the end of the continuum that comes closest to your situation.

When necessary, I am able to contradict a domineering person.

NEVER _____ALL THE TIME

When someone is sarcastic to me, I can express my displeasure.

NEVER _____ALL THE TIME

I can accept and use valid criticism without feeling uncomfortable.

NEVER _____ALL THE TIME

Bev could have used this approach when her boss intimidated her with: "Seems like you've been working on this for months." Her response to focus on the process and not address the content could be: "Perhaps. Now what I'd like to clarify with you is…"

If Bev allowed herself to be intimidated by his accusation, she could easily find herself justifying and explaining how much time has been spent on the project instead of keeping focused on the point she wants to clarify.

You can choose when you want to pursue the content of a comment to get needed information and when you want to ignore it and manage the manipulative process of a comment in an effective way.

Be your own judge. Don't give away the power to judge you, your abilities, your style or your motives to anybody else — especially somebody who does so in an intimidating manner.

2. Who intimidates you?

Do Worksheet #41 to see who intimidates you. If you're having trouble recalling specifics about who intimidates you, turn to Worksheet #4 in chapter 2, and run down the list of passive and aggressive behaviors. Do these behaviors remind you of any people you have to deal with?

3. Use the basic assertive skills to manage intimidation

In Worksheets #42 to #45, write your own responses to the situations described. Then read the examples and discussion. Check your responses and use the key tips for assertive skills to improve.

WORKSHEET #41
WHO INTIMIDATES YOU?

1. Who, or what kinds of people, intimidate you?

_____

_____

_____

2. What are the types of comments or behavior these people use?

_____

_____

_____

3. List any patterns you can identify in the type of people (age, sex, education, race), the type of relationship (power over you, coworkers, clients), the work context (selling, time-pressured, isolated), etc.

_____

_____

_____

WORKSHEET #42
MANAGING INTIMIDATION

As a client rep for a large public relations firm, you've been having trouble lately getting the cooperation you need from your colleagues in the other departments to keep to the agreed deadlines. When the graphics aren't done, for example, you can't give your client the service you want to give. At a staff meeting with all departments present, you have started to voice your concerns. One of the other people at the meeting cuts you off with: "There you go again, all you ever do is complain...."
You say:

_____

_____

Choose three situations from your list of "who intimidates you." Write responses to demonstrate that you know how to acknowledge the process of intimidating remarks without getting "hooked in" to the content. Remember you are looking for ways to stay in charge of yourself in the communication process.

1. _____

_____

_____

2. _____

_____

_____

3. _____

_____

_____

Check your response. Use assertive skills to manage intimidation.

> It may seem like that ... nevertheless, I am concerned about the lack of coordination....

> Some may think so ... nevertheless, I think we need to talk about the coordination between....

KEY TIPS

- **Acknowledge the process briefly —** Intimidating, demeaning, sarcastic remarks are like pot shots from a sniper behind a bush. You need to take the bush away to defuse the sniper's power over you. You don't need (or want) to give credit (more power) to the content of the shot directed at you. Ignoring the sniper in silence will not work. Everyone else has heard it. Even if you are alone with the sniper, you take home the stress and anguish of suffering in silence, and not being able to deal with it.

Acknowledge the intimidating tactics with a short, innocuous comment. Acknowledgment does not imply agreement. These types of comments can work: "It may seem like that...," "Perhaps so," "Some may think so," "Maybe I am."

Intimidating tactics may be nonverbal: lifting an eyebrow, slumping over, smirking, twirling a pen, etc. Acknowledge the behavior briefly, but don't address what's going on: "You seem bored, Bob; nevertheless, I think it's important that we discuss...."

If you get hooked in by the intimidating tactics and address the content ("I don't always complain...."), a good intimidator will be able to beat your argument, justification, or explanation with more ammunition. The intimidator doesn't worry about whether the ammunition used against you is true or not; an intimidator feels successful when he or she gets you on the defensive.

- **Control the content** — Immediately move back on track with a clear statement of the issue you want to address. This will demonstrate that you are clearly in charge of yourself in this communication process. Use a transition word such as "nevertheless" to refocus and get back on track.

Remember that the content is irrelevant coming from an intimidator. Therefore, it is important for you to keep control of the content to ensure better data and the potential for respect.

Now check your response again. Do you acknowledge the process briefly and ignore the content? Do you control your own content by coming back on track? Practice responses for people who intimidate you. Use Worksheet #43 to rewrite your statements after reading the examples and discussion.

WORKSHEET #43
MANAGING INTIMIDATION REWRITE

1. _____

_____

_____

2. _____

_____

_____

3. _____

_____

_____

WORKSHEET #44
MANAGING SARCASM

Every time you ask your boss for some clarification or for some information, he makes you feel inferior with his belittling and sarcastic remarks. "Haven't you figured that out yet?" "I thought I told you that." "Can't remember much can you?" He sighs and winces, stares you down and makes you feel like you are wasting his time. You realize his manner is making you reluctant to go to him, yet if you don't get the information you need, you can't do your work properly. You decide to talk to him.

You say

_____

_____

_____

Once again, look over your list of "who intimidates you." How many of the incidents described are actually patterns rather than single events with a person? Choose a pattern that undermines you and that you would like to deal with effectively. Use this space to practice addressing the pattern and stating your limits.

_____

_____

_____

_____

_____

_____

_____

_____

Check your response. Use assertive skills to manage sarcasm.

> When you are impatient with me because I am asking questions, I am reluctant to check things out with you. I need your help at times, but I don't need the sarcastic comments.

> I'm not happy with the way we deal with each other generally. I get mad and lose my confidence when you belittle me. I don't think that's very productive. I want you to stop making sarcastic remarks when I ask for clarification.

KEY TIPS

- **Address the pattern** — If someone gives you useful, relevant criticism but always does it in an aggressive or intimidating manner, use this skill. If someone is continuously intimidating you (demeaning, belittling, attacking you) regardless of whether the content is relevant or not, use this skill to address the pattern. Be very clear that your focus is on the pattern over time — "the way we deal with each other."

Describe the behavior and impact for you, for your work, for the relationship. Own your perspective. You have a right to see the world the way you do and to feel the way you do. This is especially important if your intimidator comes back with such retorts as: "You shouldn't be mad about a little thing like that." "What's the matter, can't you take it?" Keep yourself on track with, "Maybe not, nevertheless, I'm concerned about the way we deal with each other...."

- **State your limits** — It doesn't matter what your intimidator thinks you should take or wants you to take. You are in charge of your own self-esteem. You be the judge. Clearly assert what you need, what you want changed. "I

want you to stop making sarcastic remarks." It does not guarantee that you'll get it. The person may not change, but that is not the primary reason for learning to manage intimidation. The primary reason is that you will be supporting your own self-esteem. You will feel less internal stress when you stop letting yourself be abused and manipulated.

Now check your response again. Use Worksheet #45 to rewrite it showing how you can address the pattern and state your limits. Practice responses for other patterns that you have defined from your list of who intimidates you.

4. What's stopping you?

What's stopping you from using basic assertive skills to manage intimidation? Which of the following arguments do you give yourself?

- **I'm scared to...what will happen next?** — Focus your attention on what's happening to you right now and risk dealing with it. Deal with the con-

WORKSHEET #45
MANAGING SARCASM REWRITE

sequences when (and if) they occur. Believe in yourself that you will be able to deal with the consequences. You may not deal with them perfectly, but if you suppress and restrict your willingness to deal with what's happening to you for fear of the consequences, you will never learn to deal with them more effectively.

It is a risk. Taking risks enhances self-esteem and a sense of personal power. For many women, risks are overemphasized. Practice risking expressing feelings and opinions, to requesting what you want and need, and finally to refusing abuse.

- **I can't think of it at the time** — Measure the trend, not perfection. Make sure the trend is right — that you are becoming more and more aware of the ways you lose your self-esteem to intimidators. Begin in small, slow steps to use the basic assertive skills to take charge and deal effectively with intimidation.

Close the gap. If you think of something you wish you'd said but didn't, go back. "When we were discussing...yesterday, I didn't feel comfortable with...." "I was upset with the way we dealt with each other on Monday and I'd like to talk about it...." This is excellent practice for you. Gradually the time gap will become smaller and you'll find that you can deal with things in the present, when they are happening. It also signals to the other person that you are aware of some of the ineffective things that are happening and not about to let them go.

- **Why bother? I can't stand her anyway** — You are doing it for *you*. It's not for someone else that you are learning to deal with intimidation. Your first priority is you. Take 100 percent responsibility for nurturing and maintaining your own self-esteem. That means dealing with issues that undermine it. If, as a result of dealing effectively with intimidation, you also help someone else change his or her behavior for the better or solve a problem, that's great, but it is not your first priority.

Now stretch your limits. In Worksheet #46, make one firm commitment to yourself about one situation or person you are going to deal with more effectively to manage the intimidation in your life.

WORKSHEET #46
MANAGING INTIMIDATION IN YOUR LIFE

_____

_____

_____

_____

_____

_____

Chapter 9 reading list

Fritz, Robert. *The Path of Least Resistance.* Salem, Mass.: DMA, Inc., 1987.

Morrison, Ann M., Randall P. White, Ellen Van Velsor, and the Center for Creative Leadership. *Breaking the Glass Ceiling: can Women reach for the Top of America's Largest Corporations?* Reading, Mass.: Addison-Wesley Publishing Co., Inc., 1987.

GIVE AND TAKE:
IT ALL ADDS UP

The communication process is a valuable resource. It is the means to motivate and modify behavior. It is a resource that can significantly influence the achievement of goals. It is the resource that contributes to a committed, innovative team upon which a manager can depend.

The give and take in assertive skills described in this book will help you manage that resource effectively. The basic skills, as described, can be used in any of the situations that confront managers daily. Once you are competent in using the basic skills, you will feel confident to handle most situations, whatever the context.

Your communication process is one of your most valuable resources. Manage it well.

APPENDIX
KEY TO THE GIVE AND TAKE IN EXERCISES

The following are suggested responses for each of the practice exercises on the basic give and take in skills in chapters 3 and 4. These are not meant to be the only correct responses. They are provided here as examples of one way to respond effectively in each of the situations. In any situation, there are usually several different ways to demonstrate effective assertive skills, depending on your own personality and choice of words. Underlying each effective response, however, are the critical assumptions of assertive communication.

Worksheet #5: Giving information

1. My salary and salaries of others in comparable positions in this industry don't compare very favorably. (You could go on with: I'm concerned about the discrepancy and I'd like to talk to you about it.)

2. When past due accounts aren't included in the next month's totals, the balance will be out by that amount. (This lets your employee take responsibility for making the obvious connection.)

Worksheet #6: Giving your opinion

1. I think my experience over the past four years and the results I have attained with project X warrant a salary in the medium-high range. (Now you can deal with the discrepancy in the ways you and your superior evaluate your performance if that becomes the issue.)

2. I don't think we should treat this client so impersonally at this time. I think we'd lose his loyalty. (Go on to give information: He's been with us over three years and this is the first time he's been in trouble.)

Worksheet #7: Stating your needs and expectations

1. I want you to come back from your breaks on time. I need to count on your being here at specific times. (If you want, you can go on to give information: I can't be here myself on a regular basis but the department policy requires one "signature" on the floor at all times. As my assistant, I count on you to fill that role.)

2. I need some time with you to clarify the use of the new pricing formats. (Go on to share your feelings: I'm a little hesitant about filling it in this month before I'm sure how to calculate the breakdowns.)

Worksheet #8: Sharing feelings

1. This is an important discussion to me. I'm getting upset with the interruptions. (Go on to state your needs: I'd like to speak to you when we won't be interrupted.)

2. I can't concentrate on these calculations when you interrupt me. I'm really getting frustrated. (Go on to state your needs: I'd like you to hold your questions until I'm through with this report.)

Worksheet #9: Giving your decision

1. Yes response: Yes, I will make an arrangement to adjust the dates. (Go on with stating your needs: I need you to give me the changes in writing.)

No response: No, I won't change vacation dates now. (I understand your disappointment. I'd like to help you but I won't change the dates.) (Keep focused under pressure. Go on to give information if you wish.)

2. No, I won't have an extra typist for you this morning. (Go on to give your opinion: I don't

agree with your counting on my department to take care of your overload. I don't think it solves the real problem. I'll support you with looking at your department's staffing problems if you want my help.)

Worksheet #10: Giving compliments or criticism

1. Bob and Dave can't start their day's work before you arrive to set the machines. When you are late, they lose time on the project. (Go on to state your needs: I'd like you to arrive on time in the morning.)

2. Pleased response: The graphs you've prepared are spaced and colored perfectly for overhead transparencies. I'm really pleased with your work.

Displeased response: I can't use the graphs you've prepared for overhead transparencies because the print is too small and they are too crowded. (Go on to state needs: I'd like you to redo them.)

Worksheet #11: Seeking information

1. How could we guarantee a supply of the standard items in the supply cupboard? (This will get you the most information the fastest way. Beginning with, Who orders? or When? are okay but slower. Bring the clerk in on the problem solving right away.)

2. How could we reduce the rejects we're getting on the new machines? (It's tempting to ask a why question in these situations but you'll create a defensive reaction with it, and receive little or no real information.)

Worksheet #12: Reflecting content

1. Two different interpretations to reflect content:

   (a) Sounds like you've been getting the runaround with this client, is that right?

   (b) Seems like our client account load is more of a job than it used to be, is that what you mean?

2. Two different interpretations to reflect content:

   (a) You seem to be concerned about whether others will have a fair evaluation of what you can do, is that it?

   (b) Sounds like there's some confusion over whom you should be listening to, is that right?

Worksheet #13: Reflecting feelings

1. Two different interpretations:

   (a) Boy, you seem to be fed up with the lack of understanding others have about these new machines.

   (b) Sounds like you're concerned you're going to be blamed for late runs on these new machines, is that it?

2. Two different interpretations:

   (a) You're pretty discouraged about the lack of support you're getting, aren't you?

   (b) It must be frustrating for you to see your best people move on once you've got to know them.

Worksheet #14: Taking in criticism

1. What is it about the timing that makes it a problem? (Explore it.)

I know. I blew it. I gave in to their pressure. (Own it.) (Go on to seek information: How could I help you bail out?)

2. What was it about the state of my plan that makes it seem I lucked out? (Explore it.)

It must seem like that. (Ignore it.)

Worksheet #15: Taking in compliments

1. Thank you. I'm glad I could help.

2. Thank you. I appreciate your telling me.

Worksheet #16: Modeling flexibility

1. You're right. Now that I see it in print, it is easier for our field staff to use this format. That's critical.

2. I'd like to support your requests for some better career planning information. I've learned some things about using career planning and I can see now how some of these activities and discussions can benefit all of us. (Go on to give information.)